THE
Gorilla Diaries

A companion book to
Tales from Gorilla Girl

The Magic and Mystery of My Life With Animals

A N N   S O U T H C O M B E

ISBN: 978-0-9983677-9-8

Cover and interior designer Deborah Perdue
Editor H. Ní Aódagaín

Published by
Applegate Valley Publishing
Grants Pass, Oregon
www.applegatevalleypublishing.com

www.atrans-specieslife.com/

Dedication

*I dedicate these stories to all those who care for gorillas
in captivity to make sure they live meaningful lives.*

*And to those who work hard to ensure that gorillas
continue to thrive, in their natural habitat .*

I began living my dream job when I became a "gorilla mom" at the Cincinnati Zoo in 1970.

Introduction

Since my earliest memories, I have always wanted to work with animals. I was happiest being with my dog or saving injured animals. I had a strong desire, even as a kid, to be of service and an advocate for animals, especially animals in captivity. I wanted to make their lives better. I began living my dream job when I became a "gorilla mom" at the Cincinnati Zoo in 1970. I was twenty-three years old, and beginning my careeer of forty years in service to animals. My book, *Tales From Gorilla Girl, the Magic and Mystery of my Life with Animals*, describes some of my experiences, and the special animals I loved and took care of.

Being a "gorilla mom" meant I was in charge of the care and well-being of the baby gorillas who were born at the zoo, but who had been taken from their moms for various reasons. From 1970 until 1977, I had the privilege to nurture, cuddle, and play with these fascinating gorillas. By 1977, I was in charge of seven gorillas, ranging in ages from three to seven years of age. Though I was extremely lucky to have had these experiences with baby gorillas, a diary such as this is rare in today's zoo world. Most baby gorillas born in captivity since the early 1980's have been either raised by their mothers or briefly cared for by humans, and then given back to adult gorillas. This is best for the natural development of the babies and to help gorillas in captivity be as normal as possible. Even though it is very sad these baby gorillas had to be raised by humans, I hope that by reading these diaries, you will become cognizant of the many human-like behaviors gorillas have. Perhaps you will be inspired to help save them and their environment. Then, maybe their childhoods, as human-raised gorillas, will not be in vain.

In early zoo days, because of the unnatural and unsuitable conditions animals were raised in, gorillas rarely gave birth. When they did, it was dangerous to let mothers keep their babies. The moms were either afraid of the babies, or, because of the lack of seeing other mothers raise babies, they didn't know how to care for them. Mothers would play too rough with them; babies could also be harmed due to fear or boredom.

I have mixed feelings about zoos. I wish we humans had never felt the need to capture wild animals to display them. But zoos exist, so they need to be the best they can be for their animals. I have seen first-hand the evolution of zoos from bar cages, with no thought of the intelligence and emotional needs of the animals, to creating larger enclosures with more attention given to how they would live in the wild. Many modern zoos build enclosures to mimic natural areas and hire animal behaviorists to design enrichment programs to keep the minds of the animals active. In the 1970s, I knew this should be a priority but I was largely ignored. What most visitors don't see when visiting a zoo are the relationships between the animals and the keepers. Zoo animals have been in captivity for so many generations that many have lost their fear of humans and see their caregivers more like friends than their wild counterparts would. They are also dependent on humans for food, clean areas, and medical attention. The keepers walk a fine line where they are bonded, trusted friends with the animals, while giving them the time and space to be with their family groups and be who they were meant to be. Zoos today are saving animals from becoming extinct and actually reintroducing them back to the wild, where their numbers are declining.

In the 1970s, zoos were beginning to understand the importance of mother-raised gorillas. I remember an incident at the Central Park Zoo in 1972: a baby, raised by her mother, broke her arm. The baby had to be taken from the mom and put in the medical care of the nearby Bronx Zoo because they had a better veterinary care facility. As Pattycake, the baby, was healing in their care, a custody battle began between the two zoos. The Central Park Zoo, who owned the baby, wanted to give her back to the mother. The zoo caring for her felt the baby would be harmed and wanted to continue to human-raise her. A primate expert, Ron Nadler, from Yerkes Primate Center was called in for advice. I had been corresponding with him for several years about my gorillas. He called me asking for my opinion. I told him I would like to see Pattycake go back to her real mom. She was eventually reunited and successfully raised by her gorilla parents.

In 1930, the first gorilla held in captivity, Massa, was captured in the wilds of Ghana at an early age. He was brought to the United States to be a pet for an eccentric woman in Brooklyn. When he became too hard to handle, he was sold to the Philadelphia Zoo. The first gorilla born in captivity was Colo at the Columbus Zoo in 1956. In 1970, when the first gorillas at the Cincinnati Zoo were born, there were three hundred and fifty-four gorillas in captivity. By the seventies there had been approximately twenty-eight gorilla births, most of them raised by humans.

As I began to re-read these diaries, I was reminded that one of the most important skills for raising gorillas is discipline! It took several months of working with my baby gorillas before I was aware of how important discipline was in order to have well-behaved gorillas. It was essential because having so many extremely strong, intelligent animals in a small area could be dangerous for them and me. The first time I felt the need to swat one on the rear end, I was devastated. Even at six months of age, they could be quite a handful. Not only were they physically strong, they could give a hurtful bite. When the young gorillas Sam and Samantha were about fifteen months old, they were getting strong and stubborn. For discipline, I was only using a stern "no" or putting them in time out, a place outside their cage to be by themselves. One day, Samantha got out and was getting into a cabinet full of medical supplies. I yelled for her to stop and she didn't. I took her by the hand to lead her back to her cage and she bit me. I gave her a swat on the butt and put her back in her cage. She had a shocked look on her face! It was time for me to go home, so I just left her with Sam without a normal good-bye hug. When I got home, I felt so bad that I drove back to the zoo (a thirty minute drive). I went into their cage and she ran to me. I sat down and hugged her while I cried.

The reason discipline is an important part of gorilla care is that gorillas live in social groups where dominance is important. I had to be dominant or they could have become uncontrollable. I found that strong voice and even a gorilla warning bark worked most of the time, but I also had to back that up with a bonk on the nose or slap on the butt. When I had four in the nursery at the same time, all different ages, I had to have good control or the nursery would have been destroyed! (2017 note: I tried to use only my stern voice and gorilla threat vocalizations hoping I wouldn't have to use any physical reprimands. Gorillas in the wild only use their dominant presence and vocalizations. But this didn't always work. These little babies were not in the wild and I had too many for one mom! There were also too many dangerous conditions not in natural environments (medicines, other animals near by who could harm them). The occasional swat seemed warranted for their safety.)

My day always started with motherly anticipation of seeing all my "kids". There was always a variety of creatures waiting for my attention, as I also cared for all the motherless babies born at the zoo. When I walked into the nursery, my kids were anxiously waiting their morning breakfast and wanting attention. Sometimes my "family" included tigers, lions, lemurs,

4

and bears. The constant I had throughout my almost seven years at the Cincinnati Zoo were the baby gorillas. They became my children. One Mother's Day, I received flowers from the zoo's PR department!

When I first began working in the nursery, I had a small gorilla family, Sam and Samantha, age six months old. Their "home-base" was a 5-foot long, 3-foot wide, 3-foot high baby bed. The sides were wooden slats with wooden head and backboards. We made a wooden-framed metal screen "lid" for the top to keep these professional climbers from getting out. Every morning as I entered the nursery to start my day, they were in desperate need of hugs. Normally little ones like this would be clinging to their mothers all night. At least they had each other to cuddle with, but I was still their Mom and they needed a Mom's loving attention. When I unlatched the top of their bed, they were out and clinging to me before I could finish the procedure. I carried them around together while I fixed their bottles. It wasn't as hard as holding two humans because gorillas are natural clingers. They have to be because their mothers move about using their hands and feet with them attached. With twins like I had, a mother could hold one in one arm while the other would either cling to her belly hair or hold on to her back. I would try to hold the two of them for a while, but when I needed both hands I had to put them on the floor where they would each cling to a leg. It wasn't as easy for them to cling to my shirt as it would be to cling to hair like a real mother gorilla would have! When feeding them, I would sit in a chair with them on my lap and hold a bottle in each hand. Once their bellies were full, I was able to put them back in their enclosed bed. They did fuss for a while, but then cuddled with each other or played with blankets and toys. I then could take care of the other critters and chores.

So went my daily routine, feeding babies and cleaning cages. I experienced the joys of being a "mom" to these two wonderful gorillas until they were a few months past one year old. Then I was blessed with Ramses the First, King Tut and Penny's son. King Tut and Penny, along with Hatari and

Mahari, were the two sets of parents of the baby gorillas at the zoo. Penny was always afraid of her babies so Ramsey was taken as soon as possible and brought to the nursery. He was my first newborn gorilla. What a beautiful sight! We bonded right away; he became special to me. Sam and Samantha were also very special but they did have each other for companionship, whereas Ramsey only had me. Others did feed and care for him, but I was his primary mom.

Six months later, the other set of parents had a baby girl. Her mom, Mahari, seemed to have learned from her first birth that this little black hairy thing was not something to fear, but something to nurture. She was more motherly than she had been with her first baby, Sam. She nursed Kamari, her new baby and cuddled with her. But after about two months, Mahari got bored and started playing too rough with the baby, so the little one was brought to the safety of the nursery to be raised.

In 1972, when the diary begins, Gigi was a month old. Her mother Penny always rejected her babies, so Gigi became the fifth gorilla in our nursery family. As a result, the nursery had wall-to-wall gorillas in a space approximately thirty-five feet by twenty-five feet with the front being all glass so the public could view the babies. Meet the kids and enter the world of a gorilla mom!

Ramsey, Samantha, Kamari, and Sam

Cast of Characters
Family Tree

Parents-King Tut & Penny   **Parents-Hatari & Mahari**

Samantha-January 31, 1970   Sam-January 23, 1970

Ramsey I-April 12, 1971 (Ramsey)   Kamari-September 12, 1971

Gigi-July 13, 1972   Amani-January 1, 1973

Tara-April 14, 1974

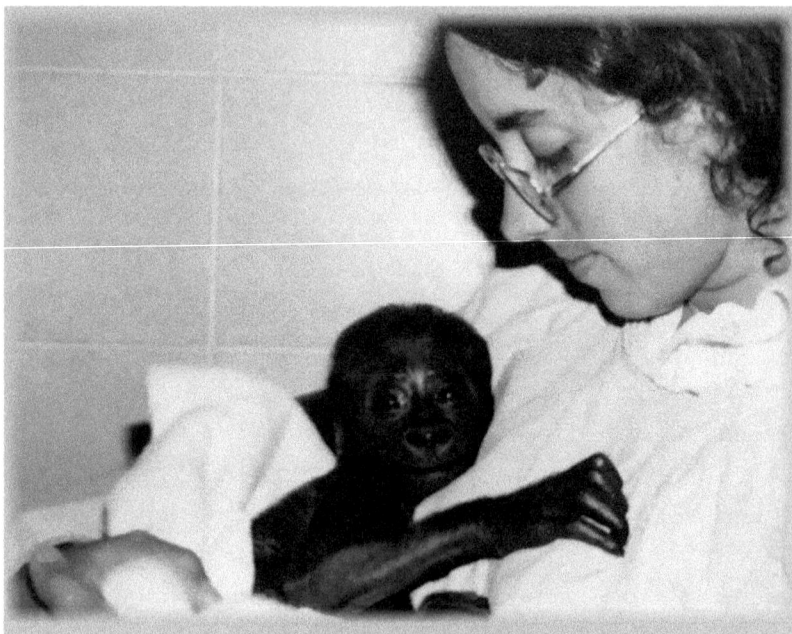

Gigi and Melanie, a dedicated volunteer

Amani

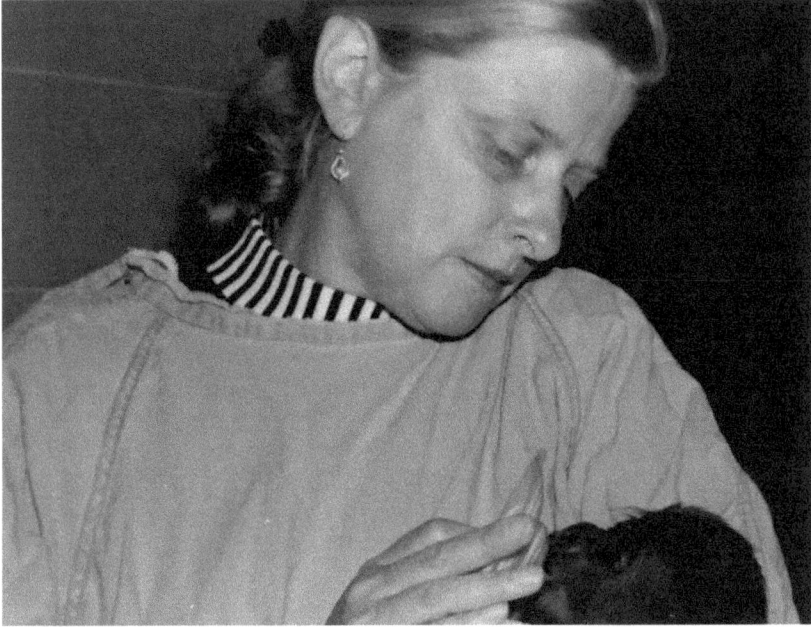

Doctor Rosemary Schmidt

A special thanks and gratitude to Dr. Rosemary Schmidt,
the gorillas' pediatrician.

From 1970 until 1977,
I had the privilege to
nurture, cuddle, and play
with these fascinating
gorillas.

1972

August 5, 1972

I have started the introduction process of Ramsey and Kamari. I put Kamari in Ramsey's cage for a few minutes a couple of times a day. At first, they were both very afraid of each other. This is day five and they have been seen playing together by chasing and grabbing each other in fun. But in their last session together today, they got into a fight and Kamari lost! Ramsey bit her and she screamed. I immediately put her back in her cage.

Ramsey and Kamari

11

Samantha's latest way to amuse herself is to hang from the bars at the top of her cage with her feet and bang on the window with her hands. She giggles the whole time.

Ramsey became very insecure whenever I started for the door to leave the nursery. He would start screaming, so I would come back to comfort him by sitting close outside his cage and talking to him softly. But he still screamed when I started for the door again. I gave him a small soft blanket; even though he has lots of cloth pads in his cage, holding the blanket seemed to make him feel secure enough to let me leave without a whimper. His big sister, Samantha, was the same way when younger. I actually just recently weaned her from her "blankie." I didn't want her needing it her whole life. It was quite the process. Every day I cut it smaller until after about two weeks it was the size of a postage stamp and she swallowed it and voila! Her need for it disappeared, too!

August 6, 1972

I have noticed Sam has been crying a lot the past few days. We couldn't figure out what was bothering him today we found out why. Samantha has been chasing him with a mischievous look on her face. Then we found them in an interesting position. Samantha was laying on her back with Sam on top, exhibiting what looked like mating movements. He was crying the whole time! Was Samantha enticing him against his will to "play doctor"?

August 7, 1972

While holding Gigi, I was tickling her as I have done before, but this time, she laughed for the first time. She is about three weeks old.

August 8, 1972

Sam displays a lot of "terrible twos" behavior, more than Samantha, though she has her moments.

Today, Sam kept banging on the front window and wouldn't stop, even when I gave him a stern "no."

He also was very ornery with a volunteer. He kept biting and pulling her hair. I finally took him to the "bad" corner, which is behind the wall of their cage by the dishwasher. I gave him a stern "lecture," a swat on the butt, and left him alone there for five minutes. I kept an eye on him but he got no attention, something he doesn't like.

August 9, 1972

Sam and Samantha were found in the mating position occasionally during the day, only now Sam no longer cries and is sometimes the instigator. They were observed together like this six times during the day. Sam follows Samantha around and tries to get her down, but does this very gently.

August 11, 1972

Today, I was in the cage with Ramsey and Kamari. While tickling Ramsey, Kamari came over and started gorilla barking at him and bit him to make him move. When he did, she stood on all fours in front of me to be tickled.

August 12, 1972

I have been trying to get Ramsey to drink from a cup instead of a bottle the past two days. He can hold it fairly well, but usually spills most of it. Today he drank the whole eight ounces without spilling a drop.

August 13, 1972

Sam and Samantha have started slapping each other during play sessions. Are they imitating me when I slap their butts when they misbehave? Gorillas do something like this in the wild, so it could just be regular gorilla behavior.

Samantha is refusing to sleep on the floor like she usually has done. She tries to sleep on Sam or sleep sitting up against the wall. (2009 note: It is too bad that in those days they weren't allowed to have nesting materials or hay. Management thought hay would clog drains when cleaning and cloth material would get too soiled.)

I always clap my hands happily when they do something I have told them to do. Today all four gorillas were clapping hands because they seemed to be happy!

August 15, 1972

Samantha started regurgitating her food and re-chewing it, which the adults do, except they regurgitate on the floor and lick it up. She keeps it in her mouth.

When Kamari naps, she covers herself with her blanket.

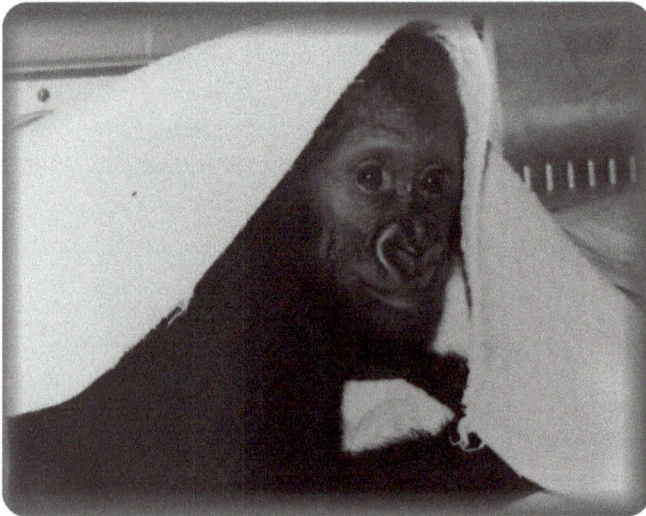

Kamari and her blanket

August 16, 1972

I was in with Sam and Samantha when Sam began getting way too rough, running around, grabbing my legs to trip me or pulling my hair. He wouldn't stop even when I let him know in a stern voice that I wasn't happy with that behavior. He then ran out the unlocked cage door . . . a very big NO NO. He thought he was getting away with it as he started running all around. I chased and grabbed him by the arm and took him to the "bad" corner and gave him a swat, then put him directly back in his cage and left, locking the door

14

behind me. He started crying loudly. He doesn't like me leaving without giving him a hug.

August 21, 1972

It was one of those days when I felt like I have three gorillas going through the terrible twos. Sam, Samantha, AND Ramsey were very obnoxious all day. Banging on the glass, running and getting into things when I let them out of their cages. Just not listening to me in general!

August 22, 1972

I have been making milk shakes (blended milk and bananas) for Sam and Samantha twice a day. Samantha makes the gorilla "happy I love my food" purrrrrs when she sees it coming. She always wants more, but she only gets eight ounces each time. Today my volunteer and I wanted to see how much she would actually drink. So, we diluted it and kept filling her cup. She took sixty-four ounces before she voluntarily refused. She also threw up a little later!

Samantha drinking from her cup

August 23, 1972

I put a blue sturdy plastic rolypoly chair in with Sam and Samantha. It is a child's toy made so when you sit, it rocks and rolls around. They loved it. I wish I had two because they fought over it.

I hung a plastic yellow toy tire in their cage with a chain from the bar ceiling. I hung it about four feet from the floor so they could reach and also swing on it. Both were afraid of it. Finally, after three hours, Samantha tried to swing on it. This surprised me because it is usually Samantha who is leery of new things.

Samantha playing with the tire.

Because we hoped to have all four of the oldest babies together in a larger cage in the future, we decided to start introducing Ramsey to Sam and Samantha. He and Kamari are now good friends.

16

The two adult gorillas were put in one large cage, so that the three little ones could be introduced in a larger area that was neutral territory. I always feel bad during the adjustment periods. My little Ramsey was the outcast and the two older ones picked on him. I couldn't just run in and help him because I wanted him to learn to stick up for himself. It was hard at first because he didn't. I didn't keep him in there long if Sam and Samantha continued to pick on him. They were together about fifteen minutes the first three days, then we slowly increased it to an hour by the first week. The newness of each other has worn off and now Sam and Samantha play together and Ramsey plays alone. They have blankets and toy balls to play with.

August 24, 1972

Day two and Sam is still afraid of the tire.

August 26, 1972

Sam has been observed trying to swing on the tire. Samantha loves it and swings on it.

August 27, 1972

Kamari drank her milk mixed with rice cereal from a cup. She was shaking with excitement. She occasionally shakes like this when she is really hungry. She is very food-oriented. When she first came to the nursery with serious medical problems, her doctor had to take blood several times. She would lay calmly while being stuck with a needle as long as a banana was entering her mouth! One time she ate two bananas when the doctor couldn't easily find the vein.

August 28, 1972

A particularly bad day for Ramsey. While in with Sam and Samantha, Samantha kept taking his ball. Then he would cry, which caused both the older ones to beat up on him. I took him out.

August 30, 1972

It has taken me a month and a half to find a nipple that Gigi can suck on. This can sometimes be a problem with new babies. Nipples come with several different holes sizes and textures (soft to hard). Some animals have a hard time adjusting to not having their Mom's natural nipples.

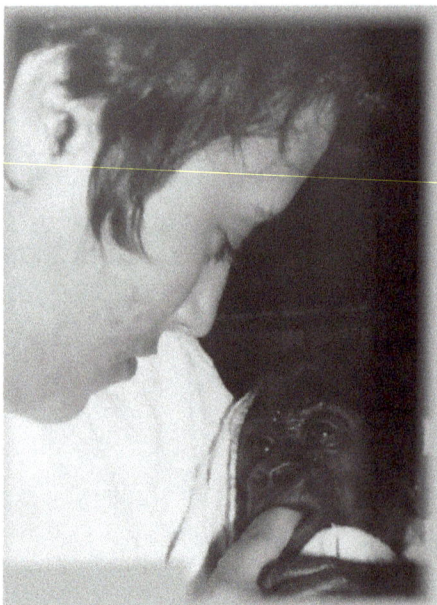

Me and baby Gigi

August 31, 1972

I heard Ramsey crying while in the big cage with Sam and Samantha. I checked things and saw Samantha stealing his ball. This time I went in, took it from her, and gave her a swat on the butt. Then I gave the ball back to Ramsey and left. All was quiet after that.

Samantha, Ramsey, and Sam

September 2, 1972

One of Sam's favorite games is to sit and slap the floor over and over with both hands. (1977 note: Both of his sisters, Kamari and Amani, also do this).

Samantha has been taking Sam's hands and putting them around her neck from the back to make him walk with her. Is this sort of a maternal instinct behavior of putting babies on her back?

Piggyback rides are always a favorite for Sam and Samantha.

Piggyback with Samantha and Sam

September 3, 1972

I heard Ramsey screaming as loud as he could while in the big cage with the other two. I went running, but saw no apparent reason for the commotion. No one was picking on him and no one had his ball. Then, with a closer look, I saw his ball had been punctured and deflated!

I put the yellow tire in the cage with the three of them. I didn't hang it, I just put it on the floor. Ramsey is the only one who plays with it.

September 4, 1972

Sam is getting to be a real problem as far as getting into things and not listening to "no." He constantly runs out of his cage when I am in playing with him and Samantha. The cage door doesn't lock from the inside, which hasn't been a problem until now. Samantha never tries to get out, and if she does, all I have to do is say "no' and she stops.

I wonder sometimes if it is a male gorilla thing. Being dominant is important to them in their social structure. He may be trying this out. He is much better behaved if I enforce my dominance by acting tough and slapping him on his little behind. I noticed today when my boss was in for a while and let Sam do whatever he wanted that Sam was a total brat the rest of the day!

Sneaky Sam

September 7, 1972

I put a toy black plastic tire swing in Ramsey's cage. He was a little afraid of it, but he will swat at it to swing it around.

Kamari is very ticklish on the palms of her hands and soles of her feet.

September 10, 1972

Ramsey ran out of his cage when I opened the door to feed him. He went straight for the cabinets and wouldn't come back when I called him. I had to go get him and put him back in his cage without feeding him. I waited about ten minutes before trying again. This time he came right to me.

The older "kids" seem to try to make me yell "stop" or "no." They constantly reach through their bars in the front and bang as hard as they can on the window, then look at me. Sometimes I would get tired of yelling at them and go into their cage to give them a stern "no" and put them in the corner with a swat, which would help for a while but then they would soon start again. I decided that they may just like to get my attention so I started ignoring them, though the sound of the banging drove me nuts. That worked! After about ten minutes of me not giving them any attention, they gave up the banging and just played with each other.

September 12, 1972

We celebrated Kamari's first birthday with cake for all!

Kamari's birthday

21

September 14, 1972

It is funny to watch Samantha outsmart Sam during play. He will be chasing her in circles in their cage and she will grab the tire swing and swing up away from him, turn the tire as it comes back toward him and kick him as she swings down. Then it starts all over again. He will still chase her as she gets back on the swing and kicks him again! He isn't a fast learner! ☺

September 19, 1972

Gigi is beginning to vocalize the gorilla hunger growls when she sees her bottle of formula.

Sam isn't feeling well today. When he is under the weather and not wanting to play, he curls up in one of the car tires on the floor.

I have to start giving Sam more intellectual credit (sometimes, in comparing him to Samantha, he doesn't fare too well). When chasing people or Samantha around in the cage, he will all of a sudden reverse direction and catch them. Also, when running around the ladder that leans against the wall at a slant, he will catch who he is chasing by going through the rungs as a short cut.

October 2, 1972

Samantha has been teasing Sam a good bit lately. She will chase him with what looks like an evil look in her eye. When she looks at him this way, he will whimper.

We let Ramsey, now a year and a half, play with a six-week-old cougar today. He was so gentle while hugging and chasing her. The cougar liked him too and willingly played chase games with him. They took turns chasing each other, with Ramsey giggling the whole time.

When he was eight months old, he played with a young lion. When the lion was three months old and too rough for Ramsey, we let his older sister, Samantha, play with the lion. Both of them had a great time. If Samantha could not get the lion to chase her, she would pull his tail and run. This, of course, urged the lion to follow. Then, if Samantha would lose interest, the lion would go over to her and bat her on the rear end and the chase would begin again.

When Gigi holds on to my hands with her hands, I pull her up so she is standing. Then she will pull herself up. She will do several "chin-ups" at a time. She is also very ticklish on her neck.

Samantha continues to taunt poor Sam. He lets her and just whimpers. Today, when I told her to stop, she looked at me with an "I don't have to" look. Then, when she wasn't looking, I took Sam out of the cage to comfort him. When she saw this, she cried.

October 4, 1972

Ramsey and Nikki, the baby tiger, love playing with each other. I let them out in the nursery several times a day and they run and chase each other all over the room. It is much like watching a young human boy playing with his dog.

Ramsey and Nikki the tiger

October 12, 1972

While Ramsey, Sam, and Samantha were playing in one of the large adult gorilla cages (minus the adults of course!), we decided to introduce Kamari to the mix. She was used to Ramsey, but this was her first meeting with the two older ones. It is always hard for me to watch these first encounters—like putting your kid in day care for the first time. Some kids are shy and fearful of being with new people. Kamari was very frightened and spent most of the time crawling flat on her belly and whimpering. I so wanted to rescue and comfort her, but I knew she had to get through it on her own in order for her to eventually feel comfortable being a gorilla with other gorillas! Ramsey would sometimes come and pull her to him so she could hang on to him while he walked around, which she would do for a few minutes, then let go and continue to crawl and cry. It was interesting because there were other times when he would push her away if she came near. It was if he wanted to be her protector, yet didn't want to show the older ones his gentle side.

October 18, 1972

Gigi seems to be progressing more slowly than did her older brother Ramsey. She is three months old and she still lies mostly on her back. She has even created a partial bald spot on the back of her head. I am sure Ramsey was scooting on his belly by now.

October 19, 1972

Maybe I "spoke" too soon. Gigi rolled over on her belly today. She didn't move much but did seem to be much more aware of her surroundings. When she starts crawling more, she will need a cage with more room. She is now in one of our

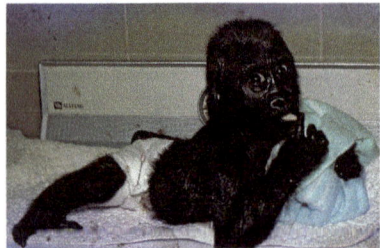

Baby Gigi

small Formica cages, three feet by two feet and three feet high.

October 24, 1972

Sam ran out of the cage while I was playing tickle games with Samantha. I didn't notice he was gone right away. When I did, I saw him running around the upstairs cage area. There was one cage with a baby lemur in it who got very frightened by what she saw and hid under her blanket. As soon as Sam made eye contact with my angry eyes, he knew he was in trouble and quickly came down and ran into his cage with us. I wanted to praise him for coming back, but didn't want him to go unpunished, in case he would want to do it again. I said, "That was very bad, Sammy," and firmly put him in a "bad" corner of his cage. I left for a couple minutes, then came back in to continue to play with Samantha. He came to me for a hug but I said, "No, you were bad," and sent him back to the corner for five more minutes. Then I said "Ok, come here." He came running to my arms and I said, "I love you, but you have to be good." Next was a round of chase tickle games.

Both of them like to climb up and try to stand on my shoulders, while I hold their hands to help them balance. Samantha stood

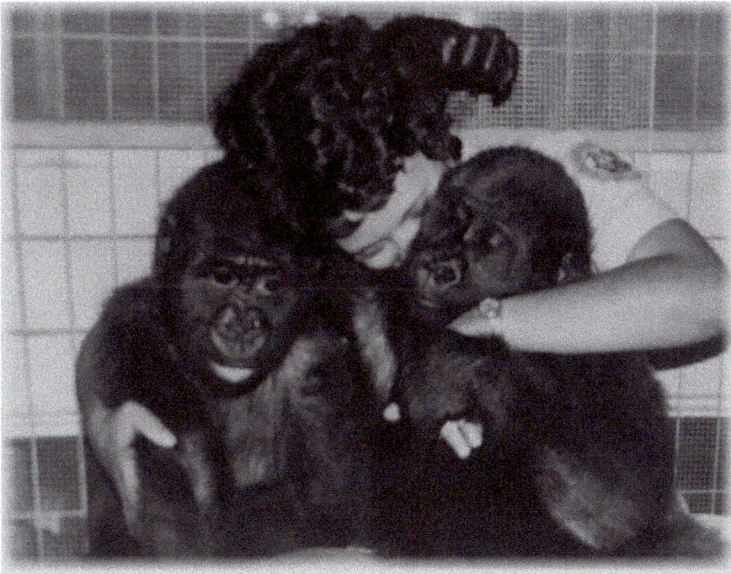

Sam, me, and Samantha

straight up right away, but Sam didn't trust that he wouldn't fall, so he whimpered a little when I tried to help him all the way up. He got down quickly. Samantha enjoys it so much that she giggles, a soft "ha ha ha" gorilla huff sound during the whole process. She will stand on my shoulders for a few seconds, then I help her down. She will run around giggling, then come and climb up my body again to be helped all the way up.

October 25, 1972

I put Gigi in Kamari's larger cage while Kamari was visiting Ramsey. This cage is about as twice as big as hers. Maybe the newness was intimidating to her because she didn't do much more than scoot around on her back. Maybe that felt like a safer way to explore this new space.

October 28, 1972

I heard the horrible sound of glass crashing and discovered that while Kamari was having lunch, she was playing with her metal food dish and put it through the glass front of her cage. Luckily, she wasn't hurt. I had to put her in with Ramsey. They will have to stay together for several days while her cage gets repaired. This will be the first time they will spend the night together.

Both Ramsey and Kamari are getting very good at sitting in chairs and drinking their milk from cups without spilling a drop!

October 29, 1972

Kamari and Ramsey have been getting along great. They even eat well together.

I put all four gorillas in the adult gorilla cage together today and they were uncomfortable for about a half hour, but then seemed to enjoy each other. Hatari, the adult male in with Mahari and the dad to Sam and Kamari, bangs on the metal door between their cages, which really scares everyone. It is quite the loud bang. Kamari runs to Ramsey for security, which, I think, also comforts him too. If Sam is near Samantha when it happens, she will bite him. Perhaps it is her way of dealing with her fears. When Hatari first started doing this, the little ones would stay in fear mode for several minutes, but as it became routine, they would just react for a few seconds, then go on with their play.

October 30, 1972

Samantha is very perceptive – she knows she isn't supposed to bang on the screening which covers the metal grating side of her cage (she is knocking it out.) She will start banging while looking at me for a reaction. When I give her a mean look, she will stop. Sometimes she seems to try to press her luck and continue to bang after my mean look and will only stop as I get to the door of her cage on my way to giving her a swat!

October 31, 1972

Ramsey and Kamari have been together for three days and getting along fine. They even eat well together; no fighting over food and they eat in record time. When they are in their individual cages and given their bowl of fruits and veggies, they slowly eat for about two hours. When together, the food is completely eaten in thirty to sixty minutes. Competition forces them to get their needs met faster!

I put Kamari back in her old cage without the glass to see her reaction. I sat in front of the cage and called her to come. She seemed a bit fearful either of being in a different cage than with Ramsey or confused at why I would call her to come through the glass. She whimpered as she crawled on her belly. She stopped where the glass should have been. She looked a bit bewildered as she surveyed the "glass" area. Then she put her hand up like she was going to climb up the glass and of course fell through onto my lap. She slowly climbed back in and held her blanket.

I let Ramsey out to play with Kamari. He helped her get used to the missing glass. He walked right through to her cage, then hopped back out. He thought this was fun and continued to go in and out. Soon Kamari followed him. They went in and out in a playful manner several times, then off to run around the nursery. This is the first time

Kamari felt secure enough to play on the floor, but I have to be close by. She has been in the nursery for ten months after being with her Mother for two months.

Ramsey and Kamari were in a mating position, Kamari on her stomach, Ramsey sort of crouching on her back. That is the position King Tut and Penny use to mate. Hatari and Mahari mate with Mahari lying on her back.

November 1, 1972

Gigi is almost three and a half months old. She would not take her bottle of formula this morning for some reason. I offered it to her for ten minutes but she refused. I put the bottle in her cage and walked away. When I was out of her sight she eagerly tried to drink, but could not hold it herself. So, I came back and held it for her and she drank it all. What was that all about? Was she trying to be independent and didn't want to be held while drinking?

I let Gigi out on the nursery floor to play in a larger space. She did scoot a lot on her belly, then pushed up to sit on her knees.

Kamari hugged me real hard for the first time in what I interpreted as affection. Before this, she hugged me only for security. There does seem to be a difference between her and Sammy. Sammy was only with his gorilla mother, Mahari, for thirty one hours. Kamari was with her mother for two months. It has taken her longer to feel completely comfortable in the nursery with a human Mom. She is just now becoming less withdrawn.

I have been giving the four gorillas, Sam, Samantha, Gigi and Ramsey cloth pads (3 ft x 2ft) to play with. The boys wave them around and run with them more than the females. Gigi and Samantha circle them around their bodies as they sit. It looks more like nest building.
I put Gigi in Kamari's cage, without Kamari, for the whole day. I am trying to encourage her to be more active. This cage had bars at different heights for her to climb on. She will pull herself up on the bar that is a foot off the floor. She can just barely reach the highest bar, which is two feet off the floor.

I have started feeding Gigi rice pablum from a spoon but she eats it better from my fingers!

Since Kamari is beginning to play more out of a cage, I am trying to train her to come when I call her, to avoid her getting into things when running around. So far, she doesn't respond well. I let her run away in play, then call her to come. After three chances, I go get her with a firm "come here" and try again. When she did come, I gave her a bite of Jell-O, one of her favorites. We practiced about three times before she went back in her cage.

November 5, 1972

Kamari came every time when called today!

I have noticed how dependent Ramsey has become on the cloth pads or blankets I give him. Kamari could care less. Samantha, Ramsey's older sister reacts the same as Ramsey, while Sam, Kamari's older brother is like her, he could care less. I suppose it could be a family trait they were born with or does it have something to do with one group having been with their real mothers at birth, while the others were totally rejected by their mothers?

I started putting Ramsey and Kamari in Sam and Samantha's large cage while the two older ones played in the big adult cage. They weren't very active. They just slowly explored their new surroundings. It has been two months since they have spent time in this cage. There was no running and goofing around as they usually do in their cage.

November 6, 1972

I switched the gorillas around again today. Ramsey and Kamari seemed more at ease in the larger cage and had more fun. Kamari climbed the bars a lot while Ramsey never climbed all the way up, only halfway, then jumped to the tire swing. I sat in with them for quite a while, which helps them become more secure and play more with each other and me. Kamari would run around the cage with Ramsey chasing her, both with happy faces. Then she would take a short cut through the rungs of the ladder and jump in my lap. Then off she would go after Ramsey. They had great fun.

November 7, 1972

I put Sam and Samantha in one of the big adult cages today. They don't get to go in every day but have been playing in there for about a month. They still aren't completely at home enough to play like they do in their cage. I think it's because Hatari still bangs loudly on the metal door that separates them. That even scares me! I try to spend at least twenty minutes with them. There is so much to do in the nursery and the Children's Zoo, so I can't spend as much time with them as I would like and they need. When alone, Sam will walk around and climb on the bars while Samantha just stays on the floor as far away from the steel door as possible. They do have some plastic balls and the tire to play with, but they still aren't much interested in relaxed play.

After they were alone for two hours, I went in to sit with them, hoping they would begin to play. Sam was more active on the bars, but Samantha just came over to sit in my lap. Hatari had been quiet for a while until I came in, which started him banging again. I could tell Samantha was very nervous. Finally, she got up and took my hand and walked around like we do in her cage. I let her have complete control to see what she wanted and where she wanted to go. She walked to the cage door and slid it open still holding my hand, stepped out (Sam now following), and walked directly to the nursery door a few yards to our left. She pushed the door open and walked to her own cage! I put Ramsey and Kamari back in their cages so I could let Sam and Samantha go back "home."

November 8, 1972

I put Gigi in Kamari's cage again while Ramsey and Kamari were together in Sam and Samantha's cage. I am hoping the more she tries to climb on the bars, the more she will develop her muscle coordination. Sam and Samantha were more at ease in the big adult cage today. It helps if I am outside the bars in the front talking to them. If I am inside, they are clingier with me, especially Samantha. When I am outside, yet within sight, they are more relaxed and can play. Samantha actually swung on the tire swing that hangs by a chain from a large metal rung of a ladder about seven feet off the floor. She got brave enough to climb up the chain and touch the ladder. Both of them have been afraid of the ladder.

November 11, 1972

Gigi stood up on her legs without holding my hands as support; she is supporting her own weight. She also turns onto her stomach readily and spends more time each day on her stomach.

I put Sam, Samantha, Ramsey and Kamari in the big adult cage today. I stood in the corner for an hour to watch. Kamari and Ramsey stayed near me for a few minutes, then Kamari crawled on her stomach to the bars, crying all the time. She climbed to the

Gigi standing

top. Maybe she thought she could get out this way. Sam and Samantha climbed toward her. When they got too close, she would gorilla bark and bite at them. (A gorilla bark is like a guttural uh uh.) Samantha seemed to want to be protective of her. Ramsey held tight to my leg for thirty minutes before venturing away. He went over to the small drinking fountain that is on the floor and began slapping at the water with a happy face. Soon Samantha came over to him and he slapped her in the face. She didn't do anything except continue to watch him play with the water. In a few minutes, she started playing with him in the water. Next, Ramsey started pounding on her back, then ran with her chasing him. This was the first time they played games together in fun. Sam was just into teasing every-one. He would run by Ramsey and Kamari just to pull their hair or nip them. Ramsey didn't much care, as he was having fun with Samantha, but Kamari got scared and came down off the bars and held on to my leg for twenty minutes. I wanted to encourage her to take care of herself and not rely on me so I jumped up onto the concrete shelf that was four feet off the ground so she couldn't reach me. She whimpered awhile until she grabbed Ramsey as he went by and followed him. She climbed onto

31

his back, but after a few minutes he got irritated and tried to get her off. She did, but he allowed her to put her arms around his neck as he walked around the cage. Samantha had gone off to wrestle with Sam.

November 12, 1972

I put Gigi in the bigger cage today (Kamari's) all day. She is developing well as she has been attempting to walk on all fours. She still spent most of the time scooting on her belly, but by the end of the day she was doing a very fine natural gorilla stance with feet flat on the floor and front hands down in a knuckle walk position.

Sam and Samantha were in the big adult cage for a half hour before I put Ramsey and Kamari in for the next one and a half hours. I stayed in with the little ones for the first half hour to make sure no one picked on Kamari. She would just cling to my leg, so after about fifteen minutes of this, I got on the shelf out of reach so she could deal with her situation without me. No one attempted to hurt her, so maybe I will let them play alone tomorrow. When Samantha would approach Kamari to touch her in a gentle way, Kamari would bark and Ramsey would come to protect her. He wouldn't do anything to Samantha; he would just go hold Kamari to comfort her.

November 13, 1972

I put all four in the big cage but I don't think they were quite ready to be left completely alone (maybe I was the one not ready!) so I sat with them for fifteen minutes as each one took turns sitting in my lap. Then I stood up, giving them a chance to leave my lap, yet still watching them. Kamari seemed braver, but didn't go far from me. Next I sat on the ledge for fifteen minutes, then watched them from outside the cage mostly out of view for thirty minutes. Kamari is the most insecure but also the youngest. She and Ramsey are cute together. When Kamari cries, he runs to her and puts his arms around her. When she calms down, he goes off on his own again. Then, if she ventures off too far from him, he comes back and puts her arms around him. It is as if he doesn't want her hanging on him all the time, yet likes her to depend on him!

I left them completely alone for twenty minutes without any serious incidents.

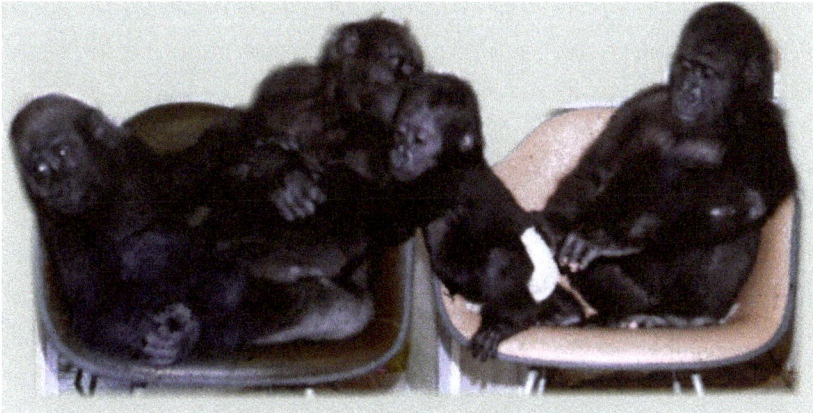

Ramsey, Samantha, Kamari, and Sam

November 14, 1972

Just when I thought everything was progressing well with all four of the older gorillas in the big cage, Sam and Samantha began behaving like this cage was now their territory and started picking on Kamari again. Samantha grabbed her leg and dragged her around the cage with poor Kamari screaming. Ramsey tried to help her, but then Sam came to wrestle him away. I finally took Kamari out. Ramsey stayed about fifteen minutes longer, then I took them all back to the nursery.

November 15, 1972

At four months of age, Gigi is my little mini gorilla. She is walking around on all fours, gorilla style, most of the time.

I put Ramsey and Kamari in the big cage first today. They had a great time for thirty minutes until Sam and Samantha entered. Kamari stiffened up and sat with me in the corner. When I was with her on the floor all was fine, but as soon as I got up on the shelf, Sam and Samantha would pick on her, so I took her back to the nursery.

Sam is really starting to test me. I sometimes wonder if I will be able to be with him much longer. He is almost 3 years old and much stronger than I am! He has been trying to terrorize the little ones by running by them and grabbing their hair and slapping them. He even tries this with me. I get angry and make him sit in the corner. What seems to work best with him is to take him by the hair on his upper arms and firmly put him in the corner with a stern "no" or "Bad Sam." He reminds me a lot of his father! He is not mean, just mischievous.

Silly Sam

I got up on the shelf and lifted Sam up to be with me. Then I helped him reach the big horizontal ladder. He was the first little one to get on. He loved it! He walked back and forth, then quickly learned how to get on and off by climbing on the tire swing that is attached to a rung. He started running back and forth, kicking or slapping the walls at each end, then making a gorilla "tuff" hoot, the image of his Dad.

While in their cage in the nursery, I saw Sam get on all fours so Samantha could stand on his back. That way she could reach a piece of wire she had been trying to pick apart. (Hardware cloth covers the bars on the ceiling to keep the gorillas from reaching through to get to the light fixtures.).

November 19, 1972

Gigi has a stubborn streak. When I opened her cage door and reached toward her, she grabbed my arm to be picked up, but I waited for her to climb up herself. When she saw I was waiting for this, she let go. She wanted to be picked up instead of climbing up herself, which I have wanted her to do for muscle development. She wouldn't come back over, so I started to walk away and she cried. I came back and she climbed right to me. Then, as I was feeding her pablum, I forgot to feed her from my fingers and fed her with a spoon. She refused to eat it. I held the spoon in front of her for ten minutes until I guess her hunger got the better of her and she ate the whole bowl with the spoon. (Maybe I am as stubborn as she is!)

I stayed in the big cage with the gorillas for forty-five minutes today. Sam and Samantha started playing rough, growling and play-biting Ramsey. He would bark at them, run over and bite one of them, then run back to me. Of course, Kamari was in or near my lap the whole time.

November 22, 1972

Gigi has been attempting to beat her chest when happy. She can also grab food with her spoon and direct it to her mouth.

I sat on the shelf while watching all four gorillas play. After about fifteen minutes, Ramsey came over and reached toward me. I put my legs down and he climbed up to my lap. He sat there awhile, then wanted down, so I put my legs over the edge and down he went. Then Samantha came over and wanted up. I put my legs down and held my arms toward her. She really wanted to be with me, but was afraid to climb up.

Sammy was swinging hand by hand on the ladder when I called to him. He swung over toward me. I put my legs up to touch the side of the ladder and he got up on the ladder and stepped on my legs as I reached and helped him to the shelf. He had never been up there to play. In his goofy way, he kicked his legs up in the air (hands on the shelf), twirled around and around, and then jumped to the ladder to swing awhile. He then swung back to me and I helped pull him up from the ladder.

Once, while Sam was playing on the ladder and coming to me, Samantha, seeing him up with me, decided she really wanted to be with me too. She got brave and climbed up my legs when I dangled them down from the shelf. Instead of playing like goofy Sam, she was her insecure self and just held onto me tightly. Then Sam decided he wanted to be with me too, so he walked on top of the ladder (all fours gorilla style). He stopped opposite from me and looked like he was going to try to jump. I was afraid he couldn't jump that far and if he could, he might end up on top of Samantha and me! I told him "no," but after a few of what looked like scared attempts, he jumped! I had to grab his arms to keep him from falling down to the floor. Once on my lap, Samantha wanted down, so I helped lower her down. Now Sam thinks it is fun to jump to me from the ladder; he does it over and over.

November 25, 1972

Gigi can stand very well while holding my fingers.

November 26, 1972

While taking Sam and Samantha back to the nursery from the adult cage play area, Samantha ran away as I was putting them in their cage. I hold their hands when walking back and forth. I used to use a chain collar and leash as a safety precaution, but the director didn't like the public seeing them on leashes. I let go of Sam to go after Samantha. Sam went back out the nursery door. I practically threw Samantha in the nursery cage and took out after Sam. I had visions of him running in front of the adult gorillas' cage and getting grabbed. Instead, he went back into the vacant adult cage I just took them out of. He was in it giggling and walking his "tuff" gorilla stance until I shut the door and he realized he was in the cage by himself! I hadn't had time to lock Samantha in, so I ran back to make sure she was securely inside. She was. I heard Sammy crying, not a spoiled or mad cry, but a scared cry. Poor little guy had to stay there for fifteen minutes because I had locked my keys in with him and had to find another keeper to unlock the door.
He was a little angel the rest of the day!

November 27, 1972

Leave it to goofy Sam. Melanie and I changed the position of their ladder and chain. I do this about every six months for new stimulus. Sam was climbing up and down on the ladder while Melanie moved the chain. Then, all of a sudden, he leaped for the chain that was no longer there; down he went!

Sam helping Melanie

December 2, 1972

Gigi is walking on all fours very well and would sometimes rather walk around than be held.

Kamari and Ramsey have been "mating" again. I last observed this exploration at the end of October. Kamari is now fourteen months old and Ramsey nineteen months. They are getting along better! Kamari will rub up against Ramsey, her back to his stomach. Then she slides under him to the floor while he stays on top. He actually looks as if he positions himself, then his rear end pumps up and down in a rhythmic motion. When they finish, they hug each other!

December 16, 1972

I just got back from a ten day vacation. I came in the nursery a day early to see the gorillas. They were glad to see me. Ramsey ran over and hugged me. Kamari heard my voice, saw me, and then came over to me. I bent down to pick her up and she backed away. I knew right away it was my shirt. I hadn't changed into my uniform. I went in the locker room and put on my uniform shirt and came back. This time she ran over and hugged me tightly! When I went in with Sam and Samantha, they ran to me for hugs too. It was good to be back. Gigi didn't seem to act any different.

Ramsey and me

December 17, 1972

Samantha was in a very good mood today. When she is in a happy mood, she does somersaults and stands on her head when she sees I am coming in to play with them. She climbs on my back and hugs me with her cheek on mine. I can hear her giggling.

December 18, 1972

When I took Sam and Samantha out of their nursery cage to go to the big cage, Ramsey started crying as if he wanted to go too. So I let him come too, but then he really cried when I closed the door on the three of them. He soon settled down and they all played well for an hour and a half. He only cried occasionally. He and Samantha got along the best.

December 23, 1972

I put Kamari in the big cage with the other three today. Samantha kept trying to get between Ramsey and her. I couldn't figure out why. She was very persistent. I watched for twenty minutes. At first, I thought she just wanted to play with her. Kamari was scared and kept clinging to Ramsey. What Samantha really wanted was for Kamari to cling to her. I left and came back a half hour later and Kamari was clinging to Samantha's back, much like a mother would be with her child or an older sibling would with a younger sibling. This lasted another half hour, then everyone started fussing. Samantha started teasing Kamari, chasing her and pulling her by the hair. I wonder if it was because Kamari didn't want to cling to her anymore. I finally took Kamari out.

1973

January 1, 1973

My training Kamari to come when called has paid off. I can let her run around the nursery and when she heads for trouble, I call and she comes back! If she doesn't come on the first call, I use my stern voice; she whimpers and comes running fast!

January 2, 1973

Mahari had a baby girl last night with Hatari in the cage with her. She didn't bite off the cord, we think because Hatari may have pestered her. The two adults now have to be separated most of the time.

January 3, 1973

Hatari was put in with Mahari and Amani, her baby, for three hours today. Hatari was very curious. He would follow Mahari around trying to see the baby and occasionally he would smell the baby's anal area. Finally, Mahari sat still while Hatari got down on his elbows to get a close look at the baby. Soon after that, he was back to his old self, teasing Mahari. She would scream and chase him so they were separated. (2019 note: It is amazing that in such a cramped, sterile cage they can still have some natural behaviors.)

January 8, 1973

While I was sitting behind Sam and Samantha's wall in our kitchen area on break, Ramsey and Kamari got out of their cage. They knew they weren't supposed to be out because normally when they are out, they love to run around. This time they quietly went to a corner of the room, out of my sight, and played with my coat that Ramsey had found nearby. Also, I had all their food made up ready to feed. It was within their reach, but too close to where I was sitting. They usually stop at nothing when it comes to food but this time, they ignored it so as not to be "caught!"

Ramsey has been regurgitating a lot lately. Approximately ten times a day, he will spit up into his hand and then eat it.

If he spits on the floor, Kamari will eat it! Dian Fossey told me that wild gorillas never do this. (2019 note: This may be because gorillas in the wild spend most of their day foraging for their food. Zoos found that by changing gorilla diets to a more natural one with lots of roughage, and feeding throughout the day, they do not regurgitate their food.)

January 9, 1973

Poor Hatari seems to get unusually lonely since he is only with Mahari one to three hours a day. Today before I went home, I stopped to play with him. We play toss games. I slide a monkey biscuit under his bar door and he tries to stop it. If he does, he slides it back to me. If it gets by me, he jumps up and beats his chest. I played about five minutes, then started to leave. He jumped up and down and beat his chest to try to get my attention and stay. I came back and played another ten minutes, and then started to leave again. He repeated his performance, but I kept going. Then he stopped and looked at me and made a sorrowful hoot cry, which he has never done to me before. I came back for a short time but then had to leave. He cried even louder.

January 10, 1973

Samantha and Sam ran out of their nursery cage today and what followed seemed to me to be similar to a three-year-old human reaction.

40

Samantha in the Bad Corner

I was angry because they kept running around and not coming back when I called them. I finally grabbed them both by the arms and took them to the bad corner behind their cage. They each got a swat and I sat them firmly in the corner. I gave them a stern lecture about being bad. Then I put them in separate corners in their cage. Sam knew I was very mad and stayed in his corner. Samantha kept giggling and wouldn't sit still. I would firmly put her back in the corner and she finally stopped giggling. But when I took my eyes off her, she would start rolling around again. When I caught her, I put her firmly back in the corner. She did get serious . . . for a minute, then started giggling again. I gave up and grabbed her and asked, "Will you just be good?" Then she hugged me. She acted silly the rest of the day. When I got ready to go home, I gave Sam a kiss on the nose and went to Samantha and she threw her arms around me and gave me a kiss!

January 15, 1973

Since I can't use the adult gorilla cages anymore because Hatari and Mahari have to be separated most of the time, I put Ramsey and Kamari in with Sam and Samantha in their cage. It really isn't fair to the little ones because that means they have to enter the older ones' territory. The older ones act even more dominant toward the younger ones. Ramsey was very frightened. Samantha would tease him (run at him and poke or slap him); he would scream louder than I have ever heard him. He did try to defend himself by trying to bite them, but they would just move out of his way. Samantha is the more aggressive one, though Sam will back her up. (1975 note: Sam is a bully when Samantha is around but left alone, he tends to be a coward.) I took the little ones out after about fifteen minutes.

January 16, 1973

Samantha is still in that "Oh, who cares" mode. She acts silly, giggling a lot, twirling, rolling, and bumping into walls. She also has little regard for discipline! What's a mother to do?

I put all four gorillas in the big adult cage for the first time in about three weeks. At first, Ramsey and Kamari cried a lot, but soon Samantha walked to Kamari to encourage her to hold on for security. Kamari put her arms around Samantha; things quieted down.

After an hour in the big cage, I tried to mix things up a bit so they might start bonding with others. Hoping if the older ones didn't have each other to gang up on the younger ones, they all might learn to be friends. I put Samantha and Kamari in the big nursery cage and left Sam in the adult cage with Ramsey. Of course, at first no one was happy! A lot of crying for about fifteen minutes. Once in a while Samantha would forget about being separated from Sam and play nicely with Kamari (little gentle wrestle chase games). Kamari would laugh. Sam and Ramsey would mostly wander around whimpering. This calmness only lasted a short time and the crying started again. After thirty minutes in these new groups, I put them back into their normal pairings.

I heard a strange squeak in Gigi's cage and went over to check. She was sitting up playing with a rubber squeaker ball. She was very content playing alone. She is about six months old.

Ramsey misbehaved tonight at bedtime. I took Kamari out of his cage and put her to bed in her cage with hugs and a blanket. While I did this, I let him out to explore before putting him to bed for the night. When I was ready for him, I called for him to come and he did, but just before putting him in his cage, he broke away (I was holding his hand) and ran all over the nursery. I had to chase him for about five minutes before I finally caught him. I scolded him and put him in the bad corner and looked at him sternly for a few minutes. Then I called him to come to my open arms. We hugged and I told him to be good. We walked to his cage, he went right in by himself.

Ramsey in his cage

January 22, 1973

Samantha was playing with the hose while I was cleaning their cage. I had it turned to a trickle and let her hold it. She put her finger on the nozzle to try to squirt it in her mouth but it usually landed in her eye!

January 23, 1973

Ramsey behaved strangely today. I don't know what caused it. He was playing with Kamari and suddenly screamed and ran from her. He kept screaming and looking at her. She was just lying on her belly not doing anything. Then he went over to her and gave her a hug and they played tumble chase games as usual. I have no idea what his problem was.

I let Ramsey and Kamari out to run around the nursery around 2:30 after most of the chores were finished and before evening ones. Ramsey is always testing me. He is almost two. The terrible twos? There are several places they are not allowed to play. He will inch closer and closer to those places until he is there. Then he gets a swat, but he starts the procedure all over again. I have noticed if I give him

43

a (not hard) cuff on his nose, more like a gorilla would, he responds by improving his behavior. Well, at least he will stop when I say "no."

Kamari likes to stay near me. If I sit on the floor, she does this little hop then plops on my lap and is very content to stay there.

January 24, 1973

I have noticed that Samantha seems to have a devious plan of waiting until I have Gigi in my arms feeding her a bottle before becoming obnoxious. Samantha will bang over and over on the window, kind of how kids wait until you are on the phone before acting up.

January 26, 1973

I got very behind today with four baby cougars to feed.

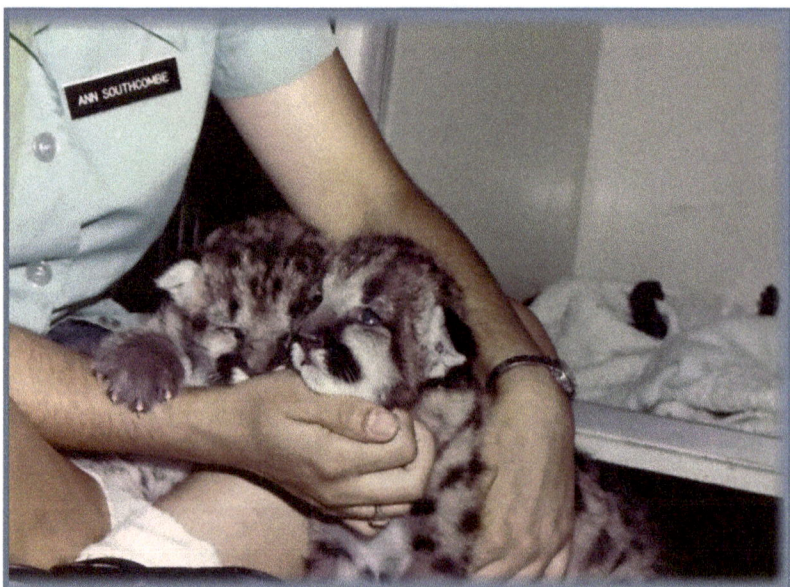

*Baby cougars. Notice in the background
baby Gigi's little arms peeking from her blankets*

It was approaching 7:30 pm and I was getting ready to go home, when I noticed that Sam and Samantha had smeared stool all over their cage! I had to get the hose out and clean them and the cage. I notice if I am there way past my leaving time it seems to upset Samantha. She is a routine kind of girl! She gets whiny and cries when I leave, which she never does when in a normal routine. Maybe she thinks since I am still there, I am not going home, so cries when I do.

After I hosed down the cage and gave them a bath, I took the hose back out to the hall (where it is kept). Samantha let out this very distressful cry. Maybe she thought I was leaving without drying them off or giving them a goodbye hug (something I always do). When I came back in and got towels for drying them, she began her happy rolls (somersaults while giggling).

January 27, 1973

Gigi isn't accepting solid food very well. I have offered pieces of banana and apple with no luck. I was told by her pediatrician to offer the solids in the morning before her bottle so she will be very hungry. I usually do this, but after a few minutes of her refusing, I give in and give her a bottle. Today I put a small piece of banana in her mouth hoping the added help would get her to try it. She kept it in her mouth with absolutely no movement for five minutes before she decided to chew and swallow it. At least she didn't spit it out!

Samantha in time-out corner

A new "outsmart Ann" tactic by Samantha: she banged on the window many times very hard, then, when I came in to put her in the bad corner, she climbed to the ceiling where I couldn't reach her and smiled down at me! I finally outsmarted her. For some reason, she is very afraid of the broom, so I started bringing it in with me and she climbs down to get away from it. It is hard to stay one step ahead of these gorillas!

January 29, 1973

Gigi still does not want to eat solid foods. I put a small piece of rice bread (cooked rice with raisins) in her mouth where she kept it motionless for fifteen minutes before chewing and swallowing. An encouraging sign happened later – she ate a piece of apple right away.

January 30, 1973

Samantha learned how to unlace my shoe today. She has been fascinated with the bow for a few weeks. I showed her which string to pull to undo the bow. She then worked on it until she learned to stick her fingers under the lace and pull it from the holes. She really gets intently focused. Once Sam came over to get her to play. She turned around and slapped him hard in the face. He went away and she continued her shoelace task.

Gigi chewed a large piece of apple and also had a good time with a large piece of lettuce. She waved it while walking around her cage as she giggled. (Ramsey did the same thing with his first lettuce leaf). Then she chewed it and spit it out! The waving around reminded me of the way wild gorillas run waving leafy branches.

I put a fifteen-gallon plastic tub of water in with Sam and Samantha to see if they would play in it. They circled it for a while, then Samantha started splashing in it, scooping some up to her mouth and finally got the nerve to sit in it. Once they both got used to it, they had a great time running and jumping in it or just splashing water all over themselves. (1974 note: When Ramsey and Kamari were old enough, they liked to too!)

Ramsey and Kamari playing with tub of water

Both Sam and Samantha love playing with me while I am on all fours like another gorilla. Samantha likes to ride around on my back and Sam likes to jump up and down on me!

January 31, 1973

We had a "Happy Birthday" party for Sam and Samantha . . . three years old! The press came and we got five gorillas around a cake (a nearly impossible feat!). Ramsey was the only one who touched it. The rest wanted to destroy the camera equipment. (I held Gigi.) When I took all the gorillas out except Sam and Samantha, they finally destroyed the cake! Lots of fun!

Samantha and me covered in birthday cake

February 3, 1973

Sammy played the game I play with his father, Hatari. I roll an object under his cage bars and he tries to stop it and roll it back to me. He makes the happy grrrrr sounds as he plays. Samantha seemed jealous (doesn't like the game) and tried to get Sam to play with her, but he continued to focus on our game.

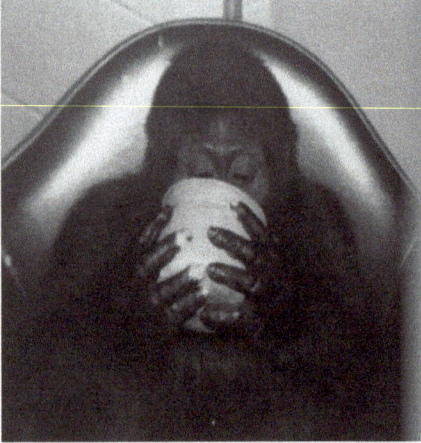

Kamari drinking from cup

February 4, 1973

All the gorillas except Gigi are drinking from cups very well. They all prefer for me to hold the cup but it is much easier for me to have them drink by themselves! Sometimes Ramsey will refuse to hold his because he likes to be pampered.

I let Gigi out to explore on her own. She was very sure of herself and ventured about six feet from me without her blanket!

February 5, 1973

Sam is getting so strong; he can grab me around my neck (when I am on all fours) and pull me around the cage! I try acting like him, making play vocalizations, then grabbing him in the same way. (1975 note: I later found this is not a good idea to play the way they do. It only encourages them to treat me as a gorilla which causes trouble as they get stronger. It is best to play as gently as possible and teach them they only play rough with each other.)

February 7, 1973

Gigi gets so excited when she is allowed out on her own, she starts shaking.

Sam and Samantha are so much fun to play with; I see how different they are. When Samantha sees me coming to play, she giggles. When I get in the cage, she loves for me to get on my hands and knees so she can get on my back. She lies down with her arms and legs dangling as I bounce her up and down. She is giggling the whole time. She also loves me to chase and catch her to be tickled.

48

Sam is mostly a show off and runs around being tough. He runs by and grabs me. I try to ignore the rough stuff.

Ramsey is getting very dependent on his blanket. He will cry when he doesn't have it. I don't want him so dependent that I can't take it to be washed without having a replacement right there. I also didn't want him to get in the habit of screaming for everything he wants. I decided to have him ask for things by shaking my hand to get what he wants. Of course, for him, it is doing what he is told and he likes to be stubborn and refuse. He is getting too spoiled . . . by me! Because he was my first from birth, I notice I do let him get away with things the others didn't! So, I had his blanket and asked him to shake my hand for it. I showed him six times what I was asking before he finally got it. But then, when I showed him the blanket and asked to shake, he would look away. He would even start to put his hand out and when I smiled, giving him another chance, he would then put it behind him! So, I walked away; he screamed. (My comment a few years later: This method instills that I was the dominant family member which is much more important to gorilla social structure than humans. With human children, you can explain why it is important to do what they are told instead of, "Just do it because I'm the mom!")

I then tried this with Kamari using a piece of apple as a reward instead of a blanket. She doesn't like blankets like Ramsey. It took me four tries to get her to understand what I was asking, but then she did it right away. She is less stubborn than Ramsey.

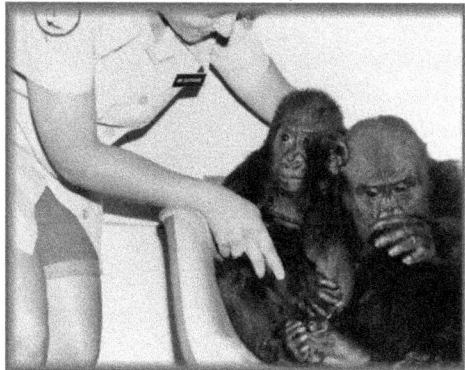

Trying to settle Kamari and Ramsey together in a chair

I worked with Ramsey again, and this time, when he was just about to shake my hand, he slapped it and backed away! I sent him back to his cage with toys, food, but no blanket. Six hours later I offered it again. He gave me a sloppy handshake; he got his blanket.

49

February 19, 1973

I should have just given up with the handshake quest with Ramsey because it became a battle of who is more stubborn, him or me. I tried today having him shake for food. We went round and round with me offering food for a shake and him refusing. Finally, I left the room as if I was leaving for the day, with his blanket. That was the final straw for us both. I came back in five minutes. He ran to me when I opened his door, shook my hand; we hugged with his blanket in between us. I felt like an ogre!

February 20, 1973

Ramsey was in a stubborn streak this morning. We had a few training sessions for his apple and milk. Eventually, he reluctantly gave in. By evening, he was coming eagerly for shakes and was even responding better to "no" when starting to get into trouble. Maybe it was a male dominant thing; once I outlasted him, all was in the right order again! He was sweeter too.

February 21, 1973

Ramsey was very good today.

Sweet Ramsey

February 24, 1973

I have been off all weekend and am the only one who works with the gorillas (others only feed and clean them). Ramsey remembered to shake my hand for his blanket. I tried making all four gorillas shake for their oranges. I think this may serve two purposes. One, it sort of makes them do something for food similar to having to find it in the wild, and two, it helps me be dominant so they respect me as the "leader."

All did very well except Ramsey. He saw all the others do it before him and when his turn came, he withdrew his hand and started sucking on it. I felt this wasn't a refusal to be dominant but more of a "don't make me." He seemed upset. So, I helped him shake hands and gave him the orange.

Samantha surprised me today. When I gave Sam some medicine out of a spoon, she grabbed the spoon and ran. I went over to her and asked for her to give it to me and she DID! A first for her to hand me something on my first request!

February 27, 1973

Sam and Samantha are getting more gorilla-like and rougher in their play. They are three years old. Samantha's favorite thing to do when I come in is to sit on the ladder about four feet off the ground. She does her happy growl and holds her arms straight out toward me. When I get near, she pushes me away and giggles. She keeps this up until she pushes me too hard and I have to say, "be nice." Then she hugs me, but starts all over again. Of course, I go along with it.

Sam growls his happy growl, kicks up his heels and then runs into me, or runs by and grabs my leg to try to pull it out from under me. He is especially rough when strangers are around, knowing he won't get reprimanded in front of them.

March 5, 1973

Gigi loves to play on the floor. I think she enjoys being out of her small cage too. She is approximately eight months old and very active.

She claps hands with me (when I clap my hands, she claps hers) and beats on her chest. She learned the word "no" very quickly. She was licking a dirty spot on the floor and I yelled a stern "no." I repeated it three times before she stopped. Then I said, "good girl." After that, she stopped after the first "no" when doing something she shouldn't.

March 6, 1973

While Gigi was out playing, I let Ramsey and Kamari out too. Gigi wasn't afraid of them at all. She tried hard to catch Kamari, but Kamari was too fast. Neither of the older ones paid much attention to Gigi; they just chased each other. Soon Gigi gave up and came to me and climbed on my lap to watch them.

March 7, 1973

As I started to tie my shoe while playing with Sam and Samantha, Samantha, who is fascinated with shoestrings, came over to untie them. I let her try. She concentrated very hard and was deliberate in her movements. She worked as if she wasn't just concentrating on what she was doing in the moment, but working to achieve a goal. The goal was to take the laces out of the shoe. She finally got one lace out and played with it for thirty minutes, swinging it up and down and running with it. If Sam would try to get it, she would run away in play. But if Sam got really insistent, she would get mad and make a warning gorilla bark at him. Then he would leave her alone.

I have been watching Kamari for the past two weeks taking Ramsey's blanket (while the two are together in his cage), stick it through the cage and hand it to Samantha, who is in with Sam in their cage nearby. At first, I thought Kamari was just playing with it herself, sticking it through for fun and Samantha just grabbed it. But then I noticed it was just too deliberate. I saw Samantha walk closer to the little ones' cage, then Kamari reached out to offer the blanket to her. I also noticed that if Kamari sees me watching her, she stops!

I had to move the cages farther apart because Samantha just tears up the blankets.

March 12, 1973

Mahari's baby is walking on two legs around the cage while holding on to Mahari. The baby is two and a half months old.

March 18, 1973

Even though I moved the two cages far enough apart so that Samantha can't reach the blankets, Kamari still tries to give them to her by tossing them toward her!

Kamari has been in a mischievous mood lately and rarely responding to "no." She will not stop throwing the blankets out. She runs everywhere when I take her out of Ramsey's cage to put her to bed in hers.

When she does finally come, she wants to grab my leg instead of my hand. I don't feel this is safe because when she is older and would grab my leg when mad or scared, she could bite me. So, I worked on her taking my hand instead of my leg!

March 19, 1973

While playing with Sam and Samantha, I ignored Sam to see how he would react. He usually dominates my attention. I walked around the cage while Samantha followed with her little giggle, trying to get me to tickle her. I sat down; she came to sit on my lap, which was unusual because Sam is the cuddlier of the two. Sam could hardly stand it. He would run by me and either hit me or pull on Samantha's hair. Once, he came by to hit me, but I hit him first and caught him off guard. He lost his balance and tumbled across the floor. He seemed to be embarrassed, then just moped around a few minutes before sitting quietly beside me. I had to give in and play with him too.

Samantha still loves to untie my shoes. Her concentration is unbreakable! When Sam tries to get her to play, she bites him. After she pulled the lace out and played with it awhile, I gave her my shoe. She smelled it, and then tossed it over her head. She picked it up and threw it again. She did this over and over. Then I gave her my sock. She waved it around like she does with a pad or blanket. Next I showed her my bare foot. She was afraid of it (1976 note: Amani is also afraid of my bare feet). She started hopping up and down on all fours like chimps do when mad or excited. Once she was bending over (back facing me) sniffing my foot. I wiggled my toes and she fell backwards onto my lap!

March 20, 1973

I let Gigi and a seven week old cougar play together on the floor. They are both about the same size. The cougar is a bit more active in that he runs much faster than Gigi. She was afraid of him but the cougar wanted to play. Gigi grabbed her blanket and lay flat on the floor trying to get under the blanket. I put the cougar away. I thought Gigi would like to play like Ramsey and Samantha did when they were younger. She is much younger than the others were when they played. She is only eight months old; Ramsey was a little over a year. I guess she is just too young for a cougar playmate.

March 21, 1973

Ramsey smashed his finger in a door; I had to soak it in Epsom salt three times a day. I would sit on the floor, then put him on my lap and stick his finger in the cup of warm salt water. He would sit still like this for a good five minutes before getting impatient and start to wiggle. By the third soaking, I would sit on the floor with the cup and he would come over, sit on my lap and stick his finger in without being told.

I found the best way to keep Kamari from throwing the blankets out is to make her come out of her cage, and hold my hand while I walk her to the blanket. She then picks it up and has to take it back to her cage.

I decided to put Gigi in Kamari's cage at feeding time. I was hoping another gorilla would help her learn to eat her fruits and veggies better. At first, Kamari wandered around the cage while Gigi just stared at her. This was her first time in a cage with another gorilla. Both seemed shy. In a few minutes, Kamari began showing off by climbing the cage sides, running around and banging the cage. Gigi just continued to stare. I was watching through a crack in the back of the cage where the door meets the cage (they couldn't see me watching). This is the cage with Formica sides and back and a glass front facing the public window. After a few minutes of showing off, Kamari went over to Gigi and hugged her. They stayed together about thirty minutes without eating much, but it seemed like Gigi did improve her eating skills.

March 23, 1973

Ramsey was so cute today. When it was time to soak his finger, I sat in a chair with the cup and he came over, climbed up, sat on my lap and stuck his finger in the cup. Then he sat nicely for about five to ten minutes while dangling his feet, kicking them back and forth like a two-year-old human.

April 4, 1973

Sam and Samantha are a little over three years old now and continue to get rougher and rougher in their play. After about ten minutes of being tossed around by Sam (he runs by me and pulls my legs out from under me or just knocks into me like a football player), I sat away from the activity on top of their ladder (the one that attaches about five feet up on the bars and slants down to the floor.) I think they sensed I was not pleased with their roughness. Sam climbed up to my lap and cuddled, then Samantha got behind me, put her arms around my neck and hugged me for fifteen minutes. Normally, if I sit on the ladder during their play, they just try to knock me off!

Growing Pains for the Nursery
May 9, 1973

I had been dreading this day. Management felt Sam and Samantha were getting too big for their cage. They made the decision to move them to a larger cage in the lion house. The lion house keepers were going to be taking care of them, which made me very sad. I would no longer be with them. The night before the move, I begged my superiors to let me sleep with them because it would be our last time together. I am sure they thought I was nuts, but agreed. I brought in blankets and a pillow. It was a pretty hard floor; I didn't have a tire nest to sleep in like the gorillas do, so it was a bit uncomfortable.

At first, I could see in their behavior they didn't understand all these changes in their routine. I was still there way after leaving time, and I had all these blankets and a pillow. We finally settled around 10 p.m. Well, Sam did, he was cuddling on my lap, but Samantha thought the "great blanket God" had given her the best present. She loved her little blankets as a baby and now she had the biggest one she had ever seen. She ran around the cage dragging it. She climbed all over the bars and made nest after nest with it. She sat on the floor and wrapped it around and around her. I don't really think any of us slept well, just little naps between play.

Sam and Samantha playing with blankets

Sam with a blanket

May 10, 1973

Management decided to move all four of the oldest gorillas to the new bigger cage, which meant Ramsey and Kamari were going as well. I know they have been together off and on in the adult gorilla cage, but not much lately. Because of Mahari and her baby, two big cages were needed, using one to separate them from Hatari, the father. I was worried the two younger ones weren't quite ready for the move.

Their new cage was about three times as large as the largest one in the nursery. Because the two younger ones were moving as well, upper management decided my nursery boss and I would still be their caregivers. That softened the blow of them moving.

All seemed to go well when they were transferred to their new home. Sam ran around kicking up his back legs and displaying gorilla style (kind of puffing out his chest and stomping around). Samantha was more cautious. She slowly explored her surroundings before becoming at ease enough to play with Sam. Ramsey stayed near me and Kamari was always trying to cling to him or me.

After about an hour, Ramsey went off to play with Samantha. Kamari did venture off by herself for a while. Everyone seemed happy until I had to leave. Then they all started crying. It was very hard to get out of the cage without all four of them following. That would have been extremely dangerous since we were surrounded by cages with big cats. It was very sad for me, as I had to yell at them and keep pushing them hard to get away from me.

May 13, 1973

They all seem to be adjusting better than I thought. Samantha played well with Ramsey. Kamari climbs a lot on the bars and Sam does his usual running around; everyone stays out of his way. He always ignores me when I come into play, but when I leave he cries the most.

They are all now used to me leaving and line up for a big hug before I leave. Sammy tries for two!

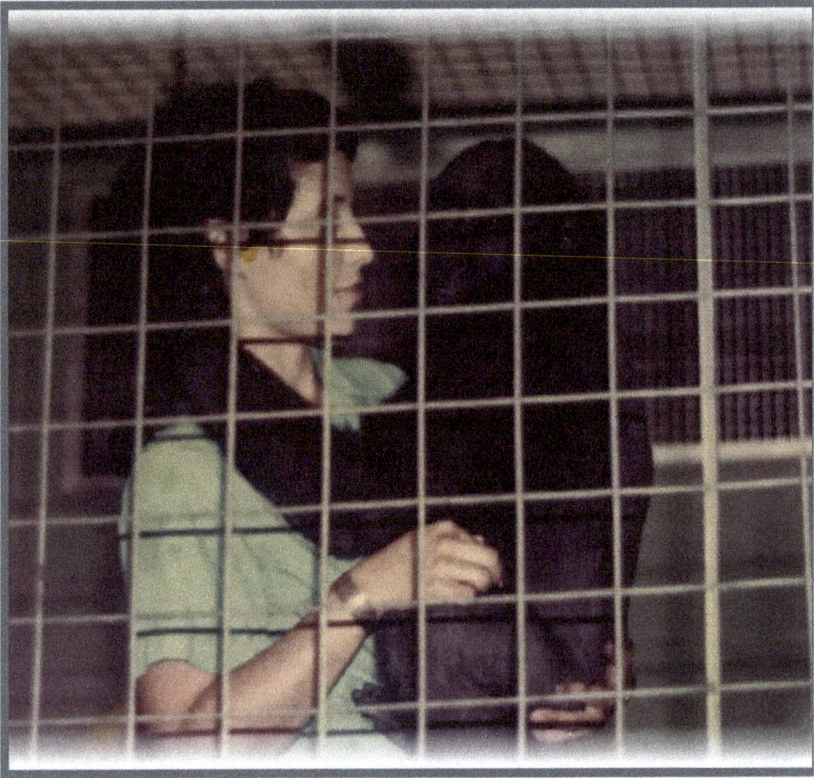

Sam and me in the new big cage

May 30, 1973

It has taken almost two weeks, but it looks as if Sam and Samantha are so well adjusted to the new space they are now picking on the younger ones. Ramsey got a pretty bad bite on his big toe. We are now putting him and Kamari in the small (three feet by four feet) retreat cage to sleep at night.

May 31, 1973

When the director saw Kamari clinging to Ramsey, he decided they were both too young to be in with Sam and Samantha, so I happily brought them back to the Nursery. I put them in the cage where Sam and Samantha had been. This is the first time they have been alone together in a large cage like this. They seem very secure and happy.

Ramsey started peeing in the sink on the other side of their back wall just like Sam used to. He seems to enjoy hitting specific things like the inside of cups and not just getting a thrill out of peeing where he isn't supposed to! Today, he even aimed for a bottle of formula I was making.

When I play with Ramsey and Kamari in their cage, they sometimes try to run out the cage door. They have gotten in trouble doing this in the past, so they usually come back when I call them. Today while playing, Ramsey's ball rolled out to the other side of the room. He looked at me and I said, "Ok, get your ball." He ran out, picked it up, and ran back to me. He got a big hug for that!

June 12, 1973

I played with Sam and Samantha for forty-five minutes today. Sam has been doing his charging displays a lot. He gets at one end of the cage, then charges straight towards me. He does this over and over getting closer and closer to me. Then, finally, he will run into me. The next time he tried this, when he was doing one of his "very close" passes, I stuck out my leg. He tumbled over it and got up looking a bit stunned. He didn't charge me again!

Since they have been in this new cage and don't see me unless I come to play, the best way to control them is to say I am leaving, and then their play becomes less rough.

July 24, 1973

The play of choice for Sam and Samantha lately has been piggyback rides. I stand next to the shelf when they are on it. Then, one at a time, they get on my back and I run around the cage. Samantha will hold on around my neck and wrap her legs around my waist and giggle the whole time. Sam just holds on with his hands and lets his legs dangle. Sometimes his weight of sixty-five pounds gets hard on my neck so I make him hold on with his legs too.

Samantha on my back, Sam trying to get to me from the jungle gym. They are getting heavy now at three years of age.

I let them play with Ramsey's small ball (a little smaller than a

59

basketball) and they both wanted to bite it. Especially Sam, he was biting it hard. I yelled at him to stop and he would, but when I took my eyes off him, he would start again. When I would look at him again, he would lick it. As soon as I stopped watching him, it was back to biting. It became a game!

A New Baby
September 16, 1973

Mahari's baby, Amani, had to be taken from her today (she is eight and a half months old). The baby had been observed having seizures; it was suspected she may have epilepsy like her brother Sam.

She is now in our care in the nursery. She seems to have no fear of me and loves to be cuddled. Perhaps she does know me since I have been talking to her outside her cage while she was with her mother. She would even come to me and take pieces of banana from me.

She likes to cling to my arm like she did with her mother. When I put her back in her cage, she will try to grab the hair on my arm that isn't there!

Amani clinging to my arm

September 17, 1973

Amani is doing very well. She is eating bananas and took two ounces from her first bottle. When I was holding her and she saw her bottle warming in the sink, she reached for it. This time she drank six ounces.

September 18, 1973

I am trying to teach Amani to play. I tickle her, but she doesn't know what I am trying to do. She sort of half laughs, then grunts in disapproval. She may think I am just being rough like her mother was. She is in the tall wide cage Gigi was in and now Gigi is in Ramsey's former wire portable cage.

I hung a blanket from the top of Amani's cage and gave her a ball. She climbs up the blanket and rolls the ball and chases it. She seems extremely happy here. It seems she enjoys being able to play and sleep without the fear of the rough treatment she was getting from her mother. Mahari wasn't purposely trying to hurt her. She would just grab her and move her around or drag her by a foot in rough play. (1975 note: Mahari has been much more gentle with her latest baby, Mati Hari. She has been caring for her for thirteen months now.)

September 25, 1973

Amani's EEG came back normal, no epilepsy. But she was very low on calcium and had other vitamin deficiencies.

September 26, 1973

I put Amani (eight and a half months old) in with Gigi (fourteen months) today. Amani ran to her and held on for security, but it upset Gigi and she bit her. I thought maybe this happened because they were both in Gigi's territory, so I put them together in a big cage upstairs. Amani climbed to the top of the cage and whimpered. I sat with them for fifteen minutes and when I left, they were calmer. I fed them their fruits and veggies in the cage, putting a pile at each end, and they ate very well.

Samantha never ceases to amaze me with her intelligence. Before I was to enter the cage, the keeper in the lion house (where they are located now) told me to look for pieces of wire. The gorillas had taken the wire off their jungle gym where it was attached to the bars. He couldn't find it anywhere. I went to their cage and first gave Sam his apple and orange. Then, Samantha came over for hers. With one hand she reached out for her fruit, and then handed me a piece of wire with the other.

September 27, 1973

My boss, Steve, and I took Sam and Samantha to a very fancy outdoor party, a fundraiser for the zoo by a wealthy patron. It was the first time they had been out like this. They rode in a car for twenty minutes to get there. They hadn't been in a car since they went to the animal hospital when they were much younger. Sam got restless after five minutes and kept trying to get in the back window. Steve and I were in the back seat with them both. Samantha was nervous for the first ten minutes, then settled down and sat on my lap looking out the window.

Once at the party we were to walk them around greeting people. We put their collars and leashes on for this. I was afraid Sam would want to take off and chase people and Samantha would get frightened and bite someone, but all went well. Samantha did steal some carrots and celery from the buffet table, which she thoroughly enjoyed. We only had to stay for fifteen minutes, then back to the zoo. On the drive home, Sam sat in the front seat with Steve and played with a blanket (waving it up and down and around) and looked out the window. He was very content. Samantha sat with me in the back seat and fell asleep on my lap. It was about two hours past their bedtime.

October 2, 1973

Amani laughed for the first time! She finally understands that tickling is fun. I think this is the first time in her life she has had something to laugh about! She seems to need to be held more than the others. I have noticed that the babies who were held by their mothers at birth and longer want to be held. Those babies born of Penny (who never touched them) want security blankets. The ones who like touch don't care for blankets.

October 10, 1973

Amani now loves to be tickled. She laughs very loud just like her siblings, Sam and Kamari.

I am continuing to put her in with Gigi, hoping they will bond. She still cries, but only if she sees me. I have watched them from outside the nursery, through the public window out of their sight, and they were playing well together.

Samantha seems more creative than Sam. She will invent new ways to play where Sam stays in the same old patterns. They both love to play with my jacket. They will wave it around and run with it. That is all Sam does but Samantha will make a nest with it. She will wrap it around herself on the floor as she sits in the middle. She also likes to put her arms through the sleeves and wear it for a while.

The zoologist put a six-inch diameter log in Sam and Samantha's cage. It went from the back shelf to the front bars. It was a really great addition, but of course it was new and different, so they were afraid of it! I sat on it for a half hour when finally Sam came and sat on my lap. When I left a half hour later, Sam was sitting on it, but Samantha was nowhere near!

October 12, 1973

Finally, after two days of checking out the log, Samantha is walking and sitting on it. It is fun to watch Sam and Samantha running around the cage and incorporating this nice log in their chase games.

Amani now giggles at the anticipation of being tickled.

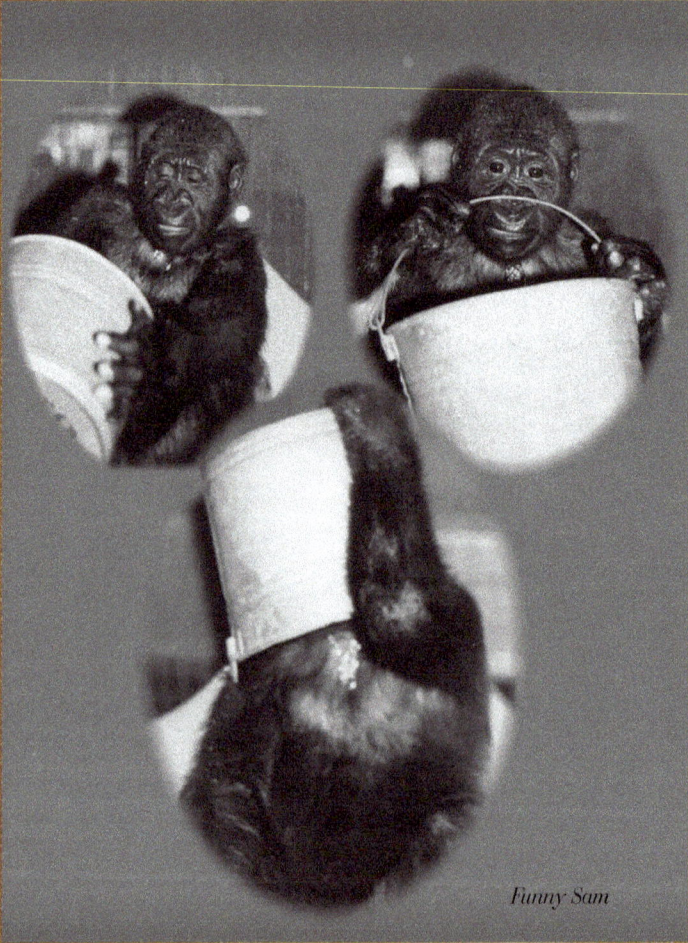

Funny Sam

November 7, 1973

I am finally understanding that gorillas must go through the terrible twos! Ramsey and Kamari are driving me nuts like Sam and Samantha did at the same age. Ramsey is two and a half and Kamari is a little over two.

They take great joy in banging very hard on the front window, and pulling up the ladder at the bottom so it will slam back down on the floor with a loud bang! Then they wait for my "stop it" reaction. They like to keep it up until they get a swat on the butt or sent to the "bad corner." Kamai usually stops before this, but Ramsey seems to relish the extra attention by getting punished.

November 14, 1973

Trying to get Gigi used to more gorillas, I have been sitting with her while she's in with Ramsey and Kamari. We stay for about thirty minutes a day. The first day, she hugged me tightly around my neck the whole time. Then the next day, I sat her on my lap with her back to me so she couldn't cling to my neck. She struggled at first (she kept trying to turn around and grab my neck). On day three, she became more secure and sat between my legs and occasionally ran to the other end of the cage, then back to me. I praise her, which seems to give her more confidence and she will do it again. Once, as she was running to the other side, Kamari grabbed her leg and she screamed. Ramsey barked at Kamari showing his disapproval of Kamari's behavior, as well as a way to protect Gigi. Sometimes when this happens, Gigi gets so frightened she bites anyone near, even Ramsey, if he comes too close in an effort to protect her.

November 22, 1973

Sam was very aggressive with me today. In an effort to calm him, I took Samantha out when I left. We walked in the back area for five minutes. Sam cried a little but his aggression didn't improve when we returned. So I gave him a swift firm cuff on the side of his face and a gorilla bark (meaning "don't mess with me" in gorilla language) and left . . . no hug, which is what they usually get before I leave.

November 23, 1973

Sam was very good today!

December 8, 1973

I put Gigi in with Ramsey and Kamari and stayed outside. I gave them all cloth pads to play with, which kept them all busy for fifteen minutes. Then Kamari started acting tough and picked on Gigi. She would pull Gigi's hair or her arms and legs. At first, Gigi stayed there and screamed but soon would go after Kamari in anger. Ramsey tried to help her, but she lashes out at him too because she is so scared. I took her out after a few minutes of this.

December 10, 1973

I put Gigi in with Ramsey and Kamari for twenty-five minutes today. Gigi took her security blanket with her, which really helped until Kamari stole it! Gigi had such a screaming fit; it even scared Kamari and she went running to Ramsey.

I then decided to bring Kamari's confidence down a peg or two. I took her away from Ramsey and put her in with Amani. Amani is almost one year old. Kamari is a little over two years old. I watched them carefully. Kamari was too worried about being away from Ramsey to bother Amani too much. Now Ramsey is only with Gigi. He tried to get Gigi to chase him. She did, but she was half scared and half having fun. Ramsey giggled the whole time. This new mix only lasted ten minutes before I put them all back together in their familiar groups.

I started playing a new game with Gigi. I show her where my nose, mouth, and eyes are, saying the word each time I touch those places. Then I will ask her, "Where is your eye?" and point to her eye. I also do this with nose and mouth.

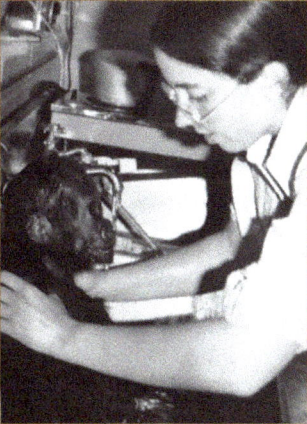

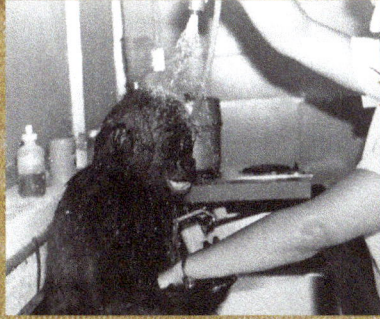

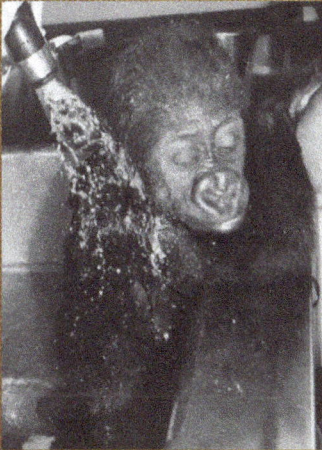

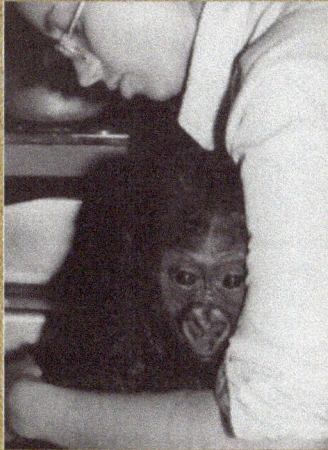

Bath time with Kamari and Ramsey

December 11, 1973

Today I asked, "Where is my nose?" She touched my nose! I asked her three times throughout the day, and she got it correct each time!

After four weeks of gradual introductions, Amani and Gigi are playing well together all day, so they are staying together all the time.

December 15, 1973

I am always trying to find ways to challenge the little gorillas, not only to see if they can use their minds in creative ways, but to help them enjoy their days. Today, I wanted to see if they could find a way to get a banana I hung out of their reach. I put Ramsey and Kamari in one of the upstairs cages so they wouldn't have the ceiling to climb on to get the fruit. I put a small chair and plastic block big enough to stand on in the cage with them. They were there for twenty-five minutes with no attempt to stack the objects. I then showed them how. That didn't help either. They seemed to be afraid of not only the new objects but also the unfamiliar cage. This probably hindered their desire to get the fruit.

December 16, 1973

I am trying more cognitive ways to entertain the kids.

The Surprise Box Test

For this test I used a toy called the "surprise box." It is a plastic box fifteen inches long by four inches high. On top are five little jack-in-the-box type doors, each opening to a different movement. 1) Push a button which squeaks. 2) Turn a dial like on a rotary dial phone. 3) Flip a switch similar to a light switch. 4) Slide a switch. 5) Turn a dial like on a radio.

I showed the box to Gigi and showed her how the doors open. I repeated it three times. When a door is opened, a little person pops up. Her first attempt was to hit the box until a door accidentally opened. I praised her and gave her a grape, so she would get the idea that opening a door is what I wanted.

Ramsey and Kamari were next. When I showed them how it worked and the little people popped up, they were afraid! I kept opening the doors and after a minute, Ramsey became curious and slowly approached. I held the box up to him and he hit it like Gigi did. A door opened, the puppet popped up, and he ran.

Kamari then came over and slowly flipped the switch and opened a door. She wasn't afraid, but left after her grape reward. Both lost interest.

The Color Test

This is the hardest and most involved test. I worked mostly with Samantha and Ramsey because they had a longer attention span and seemed more able to grasp the idea. Penny Patterson, a Ph.D. student in psychology at Stanford University created the test. She works with a young female gorilla named Koko, who is about Ramsey's age. (2020 note: This was the beginning of Penny's career as the lead researcher for the now famous gorilla, Koko, who was the main focus of the gorilla studies at The Gorilla Foundation in California.)

The purpose is to test the ability of gorillas to recognize one specific color out of four. The materials used were four plastic pieces two inches long and a half inch high. The pieces were colored red, green, orange, and yellow. M&M's were used as color guides as well as rewards.

Procedure

The four pieces were put on the floor in front of the gorilla in a horizontal line. I slowly worked up to the end result in three levels.

Level 1

I put a corresponding color of M&M under a plastic piece, then played the shell game hoping the M&M would be incentive to watch and find the correct color piece.

Level 2

I did the shell game again, only I also held up a corresponding color of M&M as a cue to which color to watch and choose.

Level 3

I did the same procedure but without an M&M under the piece. The gorilla had to match the color M&M I held and received it as a reward for choosing correctly.

I worked on Level 1 with Ramsey and Kamari for a half hour. Both did well learning the procedure. I just worked using one color (yellow). My biggest problem was keeping their attention as they thought it was a big game, so they spent most of the time hopping, skipping, running around, and throwing the plastic pieces in the air!

Cute Ramsey still in diapers, approx. 6 months old
Top left-Taking a French fry from my mouth
Bottom left-Ramsey sleeping in his cage

December 17, 1973

I worked with Ramsey for twenty-five minutes. First, we spent ten minutes on Level 2, where he got all five trials correct using all five colors. Next, we worked on Level 3 (no M&M under the piece). He got the first two trials correct, the third one wrong, and then lost interest. I let him play for five minutes then went back to Level 1. He got ten out of twelve trials correct.

Next, I worked ten minutes with Samantha on Level 1. She got sixteen correct out of eighteen trials. She got three out of three correct on Level 2. The few times she missed, it seemed to be because of lack of concentration.

I tried working with Sam, but his attention span would not last long enough to get through Level 1.

December 18, 1973

It is very interesting watching Ramsey and all the gorillas try to avoid doing what they are told. They all seem to try to out "stubborn" me! (I wonder if this is my pay back. I was a very stubborn kid too!) Today, Ramsey ran out of his cage and took the lock off the counter. He didn't come when I called him, so I chased and caught him, then put him in the "bad" corner for ten minutes. After that, I stretched my luck and tried to make him give me the lock. He still had it with him. I stood about five feet in front of him, held out my hand and nicely called him to come to me. He didn't budge. I kept my nice voice and called again several times, without response from him. He would either just stare into space or look around the room avoiding looking at me. Stubborn me wouldn't give up. I continued this for four more calm calls. Finally, he slowly started toward me with the lock. When he was about two feet away, he dropped the lock, just as I was about to get it! I put him back in the corner and called him again this time with my firm voice. He came as close as he could without me being able to reach the lock, then slowly lowered his hand to the floor and let go of the lock. We did this four times (See, I am very stubborn too!!) before he finally put the lock in my hand and got a hug! But I think he held a grudge all day. About three hours later, I tried some cognitive testing with him and he wouldn't do anything!

I worked about twenty-five minutes with Gigi with the surprise box. She can use the dial, the flip switch, and push the button, but not hard enough to open the door. Unfortunately, I continued to reward her for hitting it to open doors (something I did out of inexperience as a trainer) so instead of doing this occasionally in frustration, she does it more deliberately.

I worked in the same manner with Ramsey and Kamari. Once Kamari discovered she got a grape for opening a door, she flipped the switch three times rather quickly, then lost interest. Ramsey wasn't interested, even for a grape!

December 19, 1973

When I fed Kamari and Ramsey today, I put all their food in a pile in front of them and wrote down the order in which they chose what they wanted. Ramsey's first three choices were grapes, celery and eggs. Kamari chose grapes, sweet potatoes and rice bread (baked rice with kayro syrup and raisins). (1975 note: Kamari was always heavier than Ramsey at the same age!)

December 25, 1973

I put a fourteen inch tall, fluffy, stuffed toy gorilla in with Ramsey and Kamari. Ramsey came right over, sniffed it, then picked it up and hugged it. As he was walking away with it, Kamari began to chase him. He held the toy by its arm and ran around the cage giggling with Kamari close behind. It was quite the cute sight, like a little boy and his toy.

Later, I put the toy in with Amani and Gigi. Amani walked over to it in a gorilla "tough" display, slowly strutting on all fours with her chest puffed out, but she didn't touch it. Gigi was very cautious and walked slowly over, touched it on the nose, then walked away. I left it in with them for ten minutes while they ignored it. I gave it back to Ramsey, who kept it in his arms until I had to leave the nursery for a while and took it from him. I didn't want to leave it with him unsupervised in case he might tear it up and eat parts of it. When I took it from him, he had a temper tantrum.

December 29, 1973

I tried working with Ramsey on cognitive testing for twenty minutes this morning, but I could not get him to settle down.

December 31, 1973

Sam was again very aggressive with me as I played in their cage, giving Samantha piggyback rides. He would charge me and try to trip me or bite my leg. I kept telling him to stop and finally slapped him on the nose as he went by. That just seemed to tickle him and he came again. I hit him a little harder and gave a gorilla threat bark at him. This time he stopped chasing me and went off by himself. After he was nice for a while, I said he was a very good boy. He whimpered and came to me for a hug. I gave him one. He was much nicer the rest of our play session.

(1976 note: I recently read about a gorilla like Sam at another zoo who didn't have as much human attention and discipline. One day, when he needed some medical treatment a keeper went in with the vet.

Fun with Sam

When they tried to leave, the vet could, but the gorilla wouldn't let the keeper out. He had to stay in the gorilla's cage all night. The gorilla was nice to the keeper unless he tried to get out. Then, he would grab him and not let go. The next day the vet came and sedated the gorilla so the keeper could leave without getting hurt. No one was allowed in with him again, which is sad. I think that since I tried to keep a loving dominance relationship with the gorillas in my care, I was able to go in with them for play and medical treatments until I left the zoo. The exceptions were Sam and Samantha. I stopped going in with them at around age six. The gorilla in the story was only three years old!)

I noticed some similarities between Amani and her big brother, Sam. She likes to use her rubber ball (the size of a basketball) as a chair. She will sit on it and hold on to the bars to keep herself from rolling off. Sam is the only one of the other six gorillas to do this. She also sits on the floor and slaps it and laughs at the same time. Kamari, her older sister, also did this. None of the other family siblings have been observed doing this.

Amani is still a little insecure when she isn't in her cage. She has only been in the nursery and away from her mother for two months, so considering that, she is doing great. She has a good time in her cage with Gigi. She is very outgoing, laughs, swings on the tire, beats on her ball, claps her hands, etc. But when out of her cage, she only feels comfortable sitting on my lap watching Gigi play around the room. She will relax when I tickle her. She giggles and kicks her legs and waves her arms.

1974

January 3, 1974

Had another bad day with Sam yesterday. I believe at four years old he is entering his teenage years and testing his dominance. He is always trying to trip me while I am giving Samantha her piggyback rides.

When it was his turn I said, "No, you are a bad boy." Then, when I left and he came for his hug good bye, I again told him he was a bad boy and pushed him away as I left.

Today when I came to play, I unlocked the door and he immediately slid the door open and hugged me very hard. I came in and he played nicely the whole time!

I guess Samantha's early training of giving me things when I asked has paid off. She was playing with a nut that fell off a bolt of their jungle gym. It was in her mouth and I asked her to give it to me and she walked to me, took it out of her mouth, and handed it to me!

January 14, 1974

Gigi was in a very agreeable mood, so we worked with the surprise box. We played some chase and tickle games before I got out the box. I showed her how to open all the doors. This time I put a grape inside each door. She played around for about three minutes, then came over and turned the dial which opened a door. She got a grape. She played around the room for about five minutes before coming back, slid the switch to open another door for a grape. She was so proud of herself; she beat her chest, then flipped the switch, the light type switch. Unfortunately, it wasn't hard enough, and the door didn't open so she walked away.

January 19, 1974

Gigi was not in the mood to do the surprise box, lost interest and would not even try. Others are not interested either.

January 21, 1974

Gigi switched the on-off switch twice, then lost interest. I decided to just work with Gigi on this and only bring it out occasionally since she gets bored with it easily.

February 13, 1974

Gigi correctly turned the dial, pushed the button, and the on-off switch very well, then lost interest.

April 14, 1974

Penny gave birth to a little girl who came directly to the nursery. Tara, number SEVEN!

April 30, 1974

Gigi hadn't seen the box in over a month, yet came over and flipped the switch, pushed all the buttons very quickly and without rewards!

(2020 note: I believe having seven gorillas under my care, I had little time to do much testing or make any diary entries!)

November 20, 1974

Gigi has not seen the box in about seven months and also has been under stress while getting used to Samantha. I sat in their cage with the box. Gigi sat quietly for about ten minutes in a corner five feet from me, looking at the box. Then she came to it and fingered the dial and flipped the switch. I gave her an M&M candy which really perked her up and she kept flipping the switch for a piece of candy.

Diaries Ended

It was sad for me that the diaries ended here, I don't know why. Perhaps they did continue but those pages were lost in my many moves in the past forty years or in a house fire I had in the 1980s. I am however, very grateful for this brief glimpse into my time with these young gorillas. It has kept their memories more alive than just relying on my memories alone.

Although the diaries end here, there is one later story worth mentioning that involved little Amani and a baby pygmy hippo, especially since it is not in my book, "Tales From Gorilla Girl."

Teaching Gigi the sign for drink

June 24, 1974

We took Amani, almost one and a half years old, and a baby pygmy hippo named Libby (not sure of her age, but about the size of a very large watermelon!) to the Johnny Carson TV show in Los Angeles! Pat Derby, a famous animal trainer at the time, was doing shows for the zoo during the summer. She was to take the animals on the show to advertise this event, and, of course, be one of those cute animal encounters for Johnny Carson.

For the trip on the airplane, Libby seemed content in her carrying cage and was put by the airline workers in the cargo compartment, much to Papa Jerry's objections. Jerry was our zoologist who was the main caregiver of the baby hippo. The airline officials didn't insist on putting Amani in with the cargo, but they did want her put in a small carrier and stuffed under my seat. Since they had never had a baby gorilla riding on their planes, this was the only solution they could come up with. That's where small dogs and cats were allowed to go. I protested, "Would a human baby be treated in this manner?"

Since they did agree that Amani was too big for a pet carrier, they reluctantly consented to let me hold her in my arms – if all the flight attendants agreed. All except one were delighted, the majority ruled; we were let on the plane. The main official, who was by now a nervous wreck, gave me last minute instructions to cover every hair with a blanket and to move quickly to the very back of the plane before the other passengers arrived.

During the flight, we were very well cared for by the attendants (except the one who didn't like animals, she just stayed away). They even remarked that Amani behaved better than many humans her age. The only problem I encountered during the flight was when it came time to change her diaper, and I had to take her to the tiny bathroom. I didn't realize until then that Amani had never seen herself in a mirror. I opened the door and carried her in my arms into the cramped space. The wall in front of us, as small as it was, was mostly mirror. When Amani saw us staring back at her, she screamed and hugged my neck so hard I nearly lost my breath. I quickly comforted her; she calmed down before we created a commotion among the rest of the passengers. Once the baby was calm, I was able to change her, though it was very difficult to do with her still clinging tightly to my neck.

Jerry and I were met at the Los Angeles airport by a friend of Pat's. Before taking us to the NBC studios, she had to make one stop at Universal Studios to pick up a script for a television show, *The Six Million Dollar Man*. (Pat and some of her trained animals did the occasional television show if it met with their approval. This script called for them to use one of their cougars. A few years later, Pat quit show business altogether and only had her animal sanctuary.)

At the NBC studios, we were led to the Green Room where performers wait before going on stage. Actually, there were several green rooms. Ours had a couch, two comfortable chairs, and a bathroom with a shower. The show wasn't to start for three hours so we had time to relax. Jerry gave Libby her bottle and then let her play in the shower. Libby actually loved bathtubs best, but none was available and the sink wasn't big enough for this little hippo. Amani had a bottle and a peanut butter sandwich from the commissary, and soon we were all ready for a nap. When Pat and her husband, Ted, arrived just minutes before the show, I was asleep, sitting on the couch with Amani in my arms and Libby's head on my lap.

I knew it was show time when I heard the band play the familiar theme song. The other guest on the show, hearing that there were going to be animals on and fearing they would steal the thunder, demanded to precede us. This meant we had another forty-five minutes to wait. By then, Jerry and I were exhausted; the animals were getting restless. At last our time came. We were led upstairs and placed behind the curtain to wait for our cue to hand over the animals to Pat.

When Amani went on, I watched the monitor and became one big grin as Amani proceeded to steal the show. The screen showed close-ups of her cute fuzzy face, then she snatched a banana from Johnny's hand. When Libby debuted, they pulled her onto the stage in a little wading pool, hoping she would swim around as she usually did in the bathtub. Instead, she got stage fright and just stood as still as she could. (2020 note: You can view the show on my YouTube channel, "Tales From Gorilla Girl.")

As soon as our time was over, we got into Pat's car and drove to her house. I fell fast asleep with Amani in the back of the car. Jerry and Libby stayed with a friend of Pat's, so we were separated until we would all meet at the airport the next day. Amani and I were to have one last memorable experience before flying home in the morning. Pat showed us to her guest room, and then went to the living room to watch the Johnny Carson Show that was recently taped. As she left, she said to come and watch it with her if we weren't too tired, but I guess we were too tired, for I don't remember seeing the show. In Pat's guest room, I experienced a waterbed for the first time. I suppose that is why we missed the show. Amani and I just drifted into dreamland on that bed. My exhausted brain missed Pat's last-minute instructions to turn on the heat for the waterbed before going to sleep. I woke up about 3 a.m. in the morning freezing. I couldn't understand why people enjoyed waterbeds so much if they were so cold! I got up, put on all my clothes over my pajamas, and found a sweatshirt in the closet for Amani. Soon, the little gorilla and I were cuddling in our new warmth and fell fast asleep . . . again.

The flight home didn't include all the hassles we'd had in Cincinnati. I guess the folks in L.A. are more used to unusual passengers. Not only were we welcomed aboard with the rest of the passengers, we were even put in First Class. They treated us like celebrities. It was a great way to end the adventure, and Amani was given all the bananas and grapes she could eat!

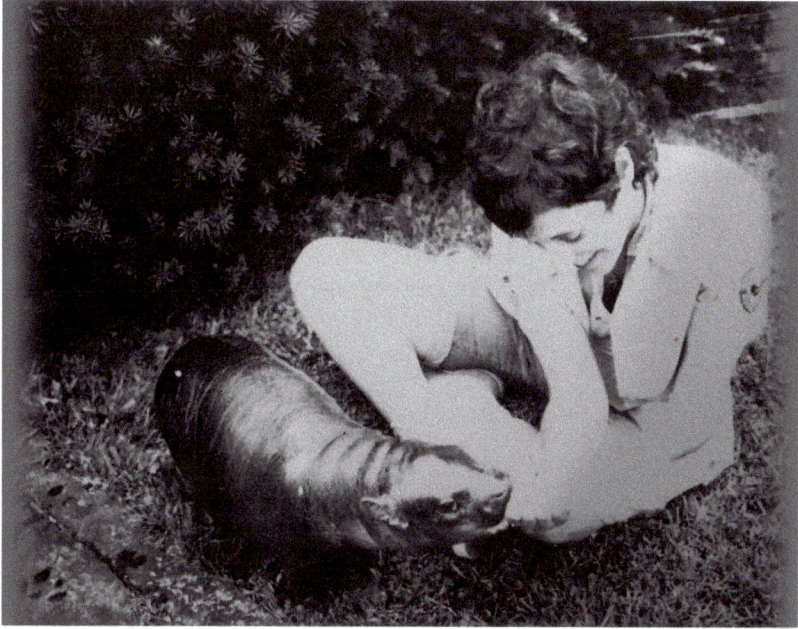

Libby and me

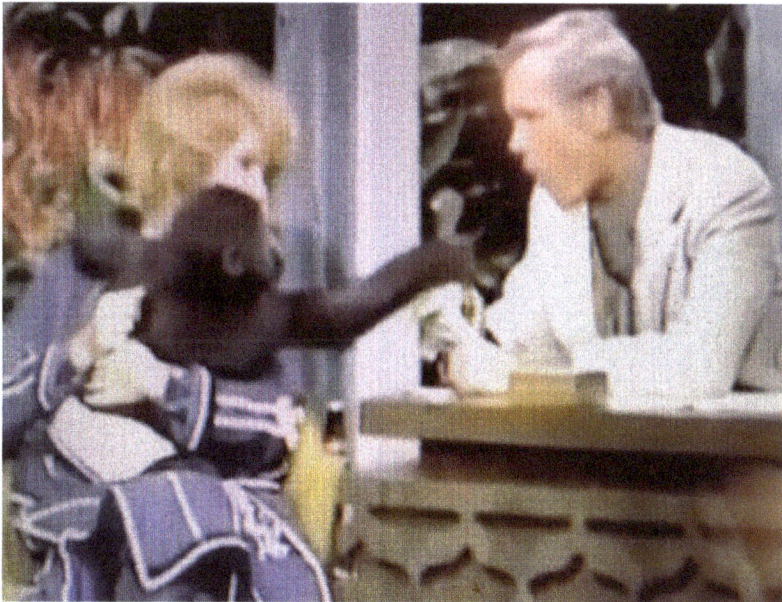

Amani, with Pat, taking a banana from Johnny

EPILOGUE

During my last year at the zoo, my family and I transitioned to the new gorilla area. The zoo was building a state of the art outdoor enclosure for all the gorillas. The babies had to live in what I called the dungeon for about a year until the outdoor part was finished. The dungeon would become their night dens, the nice cozy place to sleep at night or if the weather was too cold. But without outdoor time, it was dark and boring. This area had no windows to view the outside or the public, yet another reason they became bored. They really enjoyed seeing the public as their entertainment.

They did have toys and each other to play with so they adjusted quickly to their new life. Each had a friend except Tara. I did worry about her when I left. I was her mom, her only friend, and I was leaving. This was the saddest part of my exit from the zoo after almost seven years.

However, the good news is how the gorillas at the Cincinnati Zoo live today. The first outdoor exhibit that was finished after I left was nice, but it was more of an outdoor stage for the gorillas to perform on for the public. Jump ahead about thirty years. Now the exhibit is designed more for the gorillas and not for humans. Even their indoor housing is more gorilla friendly. The Cincinnati Zoo has created some wonderful videos of their exhibits. Google "Cincinnati Zoo Gorilla

World" to see them. It brought tears to my eyes as I finally saw the enclosure I dreamed they should have.

The zoo staff did in-depth research on gorilla behavior and habitats. Their captive homes were designed for them and not for the public. In the seventies, the area was mostly concrete with pretty scenes painted on the back walls to make the humans think they weren't surrounded by concrete walls. The gorillas knew better. Now they have a wood mulch floor with realistic trees and vines throughout a large area. My favorite part is the food hidden throughout the enclosure. As Thane Maynard, the director, said on the video, "In nature, gorillas live in a big salad bowl." Instead of feeding them twice a day, they can forage all day. The creators designed apparatuses that take some thinking and maneuvering to acquire the food.

I believe zoos have changed because people have changed. We have evolved from seeing other animals as animate objects we could display for our entertainment. Now more people know they are much like us with the same needs. Perhaps the next step will be that all zoos will become sanctuaries. They will still be saving animals from extinction and for education but not a for profit business. That is my hope!

A big thank you to Melanie Fine who gave me five albums of photos of the baby gorillas she took during her time volunteering at the zoo nursery!

Samantha, Melanie, and Sam

*I am grateful
to everyone who helped make
this book possible*

*and especially for the
opportunity to be a mom to
these seven special beings.*

ACKNOWLEDGMENTS

A special thanks to my editor, H. Ní Aódagaín. She sharpens my edges and makes sure it all makes sense!! Also my four beta readers, Jennifer Bake, Glen Price, Jan Albright, and Doranne Long. Their extra pairs of eyes were invaluable!!

When I began putting my old diaries into book form, I came in contact with some keepers and volunteers via Facebook, who cared or still care for my kids in their adult years. This was very exciting for me, though also sad when I found some had died. I was so grateful for their stories and photos.

Thank you, Angie Vtipil, a keeper at the Fort Worth Zoo in Texas; Rhonda Daugherty, a volunteer who sent me wonderful photos of Samantha at Cincinnati, (the zoo wouldn't let me use them); Gail O'Malley, a volunteer who loved Gigi for many years at the Franklin Park Zoo, later named Zoo New England; and Lin Blank Bel who also sent photos.

I was almost ready to send this book to my publisher when Angie put me in touch with Max Block who had taken photos of some of the gorillas at the Ft. Worth Zoo. I am so grateful for the endearing photos he sent of Ramsey and Amani. They brought tears to my eyes as I could see the kids I knew in their eyes!

A special thanks to Jane Rasmussen-Dewar who has a wealth of knowledge about all the gorillas in captivity and always alerts me of any news about my "kids."

Below are photos and where the gorillas are as of July 2020.

Sam

He spent many years at the Stone Zoo, and then at the Franklin Park Zoo in Boston, where he and Gigi had two babies. He died in 2000 at the Knoxville Zoo. He was thirty years old.

Adult Sam
Photo credit: Gail Malloy
Thanks to Zoo New England for their great care.

Samantha

She spent her whole life in Cincinnati where she gave birth seven times. Three of her babies were fathered by Hatari, Sam's father. The others were fathered by three males who joined the group years after I left. She died March 29, 2020. She was fifty years old.

Ramsey

He is living at the Fort Worth Zoo where he is loved by his keepers. He has fathered thirteen babies. Six were with Amani. He is forty-nine years old.

Adult Ramsey
Photo credit: Max Block
Thanks to the Ft. Worth Zoo for his great care.

Kamari

Kamari had no offspring. She died June 11, 2007 at the Fort Worth Zoo. She was thirty-six years old.

Gigi

Gigi went from Cincinnati to the Stone Zoo in Boston with Sam. They later went to the other zoo in Boston, the Franklin Park Zoo, which has a very nice gorilla-friendly enclosure. She had two babies with Sam.

Adult Gigi. Photo credit: Gail O'Malley
Thanks to Zoo New England for her great care, she was so loved and grieved by all at her passing.

Gigi was much loved by all and was the matriarch when she passed away November 30, 2019 at age forty-seven.

Amani

She lives at the Fort Worth Zoo where she is loved by her keepers. She is forty-seven years old. She had seven babies. All were fathered by Ramsey.

Tara

Tara lived her life at the Cincinnati Zoo. She was only 16 years old and had no off-spring, when she died on December 20, 1990.

Adult Amani. Photo credit: Max Block
Thanks to the Ft. Worth Zoo for her great care.

Ann and Gigi

Resources

Top Six Organizations You Can Support

The Toby Fund of Wolf Creek

The Toby Fund helps animals in local rural communities. They offer spay and neutering services, liberate chained dogs and help with veterinarian medical emergencies.

Primates Inc.

Their mission is to improve the quality of life for monkeys by retiring them from research facilities, private ownerships, and the entertainment industry. These caring folk find retired research monkeys safe homes.

Institute for Humane Education

Their mission is to educate people to create a world in which all humans, animals, and nature can thrive.

Center for Great Apes

Their mission is to provide a permanent sanctuary for orangutans and chimpanzees who have been rescued or retired from the entertainment industry, from research or from the exotic pet trade.

Animals Asia

Animals Asia promotes compassion and respect for all animals and works to bring about long-term change. They work to end the barbaric bear bile trade, which sees over 10,000 bears kept on bile farms in China, and, according to official figures, almost 1,000 suffering the same fate in Vietnam.

Wildlife Images Rehabilitation and Education Center

Wildlife Images provides care and treatment for sick, injured, and orphaned wildlife. Their many educational programs and activities bring awareness of wildlife to youth and adults. You can support this important organization, which will always be a part of my heart, through donations or by volunteering.

www.ingramcontent.com/pod-product-compliance
Lightning Source LLC
Chambersburg PA
CBHW041217030426
42336CB00023B/3374